HILDEGARD OF
BINGEN

Other HarperCollins Spiritual Classics:

John of the Cross
Teresa of Avila
The Cloud of Unknowing
John and Charles Wesley
Meister Eckhart
Bonaventure
William Law
Quaker Spirituality
Bernard of Clairvaux

HILDEGARD OF BINGEN

Selections from Her Writings

Foreword by Homer Hickam

Edited by Emilie Griffin

Translated by Mother Columba Hart
and Jane Bishop

HarperSanFrancisco

A Division of HarperCollins*Publishers*

Book design by Susan Rimerman

FIRST EDITION

Library of Congress Cataloging-in-Publication Data
Hildegard, Saint, 1098–1179.
    [Scivias. English. Selections]
    Hildegard of Bingen : selections from her writings / foreword by Homer Hickam ;
edited by Emilie Griffin ; translation by Mother Columba Hart and Jane Bishop. — 1st ed.
        p. cm.
    Selections from the 1990 Paulist Press translation of Scivias.
    ISBN-13: 978–0–06–075066–4
    ISBN-10: 0–06–075066–9
        1. Mysticism—Early works to 1800.   I. Griffin, Emilie.   II. Hart, Columba, 1903–
    III. Bishop, Jane, 1950–   IV. Title.
BV5080.H54213   2005
248.2'2—dc22   2005045974

05 06 07 08 09 RRD(H) 10 9 8 7 6 5 4 3 2 1

CONTENTS

FOREWORD

What do we truly know of the world and ourselves? Only what our human senses or scientific instruments can tell us. But do they tell us the entire truth? This much we know with certainty: every so often, there lives among us someone who seems to be able to dip into a great sparkling river of knowledge that is somewhere beyond our normal experience. Such a person was the woman who became known as Hildegard of Bingen. Hildegard had many visions that she said came straight from God. Modern scholars tend to explain her visions as evidence of illness, specifically the result of migraine disturbances. But perhaps there is another truth. Maybe we should also consider the possibility that Hildegard of Bingen was exactly what she said she was—a conduit of the supernatural God of all creation.

To understand who Hildegard of Bingen was, and her possibilities, we must understand the time and place in which she lived. Europe in the twelfth century was mostly farmland or deep forests interspersed with small towns and moderate-sized cities connected by muddy, rutted roads. Whether in town or country, life for the average person was difficult and short. Famines occurred. Disease was rampant. Plagues came and went. Children often died of nothing more than bad colds. Even the smallest wounds went septic very quickly. Childbirth was extremely dangerous. Death was commonplace, usually accompanied by extreme suffering. European society was also in turmoil with petty bickering, wars of conquest, and religious and philosophical upheavals. Might made right in this age. During Hildegard's childhood, armed and dangerous men roamed the countryside, taking whatever they wanted by force. Moors, meaning Muslims, occupied large parts of Europe. But then, as always, things began to change.

As Hildegard got older, Europe began to shake off its chaotic past and take charge of its destiny. The thousands of itinerant, troublesome knights were put to useful work by powerful kings to consolidate their kingdoms and then attack the Moors. Before long, the invaders had been chased back to Africa and the Middle East. Spurred by victory and religious fervor, the Crusades began. But in the midst of war, another reality always existed in Europe, a vast archipelago of relative peace, calm, and reflective tranquillity. It was located in the monasteries and abbeys of the grand Catholic Church of Jesus Christ, the moral authority of Europe. Looked at from the outside, Europe was a jumble of vying kingdoms, philosophies, and religious interpretations. But from within it all made sense, and it worked. This was the world that Hildegard knew.

Hildegard was the tenth child of a noble but less than wealthy family. Since her father didn't need another mouth to feed, he decided to "tithe" his pretty little blonde daughter to the Church. When she was eight years old, Hildegard was given to an "anchoress" named Jutta. An anchoress was a woman who voluntarily took last rites and entered a vault called an anchorage from which she was never to emerge. Jutta was by all accounts a beautiful woman filled with an odd sense of joy, especially considering that she had, in effect, been buried alive. Many young women were sent to her for instruction, especially in Latin and the intricacies of Christian philosophy. Hildegard spent thirty years at the feet of this strange but somehow glorious woman, learning all she could. She apparently learned well. When Jutta died, Hildegard was elected the leader of the nuns of the convent attached to the anchorage. Armed with Jutta's teachings, her own budding spirituality, and a position of some authority within the Church, Hildegard began to stretch toward the universe.

Five years after Jutta's death Hildegard was struck down by a mysterious illness and then saw a "fiery light of exceptional brilliance." Suddenly, the meaning of her instruction from Jutta and all the books she had read became clear. She also revealed she had secretly received visions since she was five years old, but doubted her worthiness to divulge them to anyone, writing that she was "weighed down by a scourge of God."

Perhaps her scourge was less of God and more of men, for this was a time when heretics and witches were burned at the stake. Hildegard knew that a woman who had visions would be suspect by certain members of the Church who believed it better to burn people on earth than allow them to burn in hell. But eventually Pope Eugenius heard about Hildegard's visions and suggested she write them down. She did, and they were so breathtaking in their simplicity and scope that she practically became instantly famous throughout Europe. Riding on her fame, she decided to move her convent to a larger venue, the town of Bingen on the banks of the Rhine.

Once established there, she began a remarkable three decades of vibrant philosophical, artistic, and scientific expression. She not only wrote down her visions but also produced songs and plays, which were performed by the women in her convent and viewed by thousands of visitors. She even studied the natural world, stripping from her writing any supernatural content and focusing on how nature actually worked, including making note of a variety of herbal and folk medicines. She described plants and animals in exquisite detail, including the human animal, even going as far as describing the pleasurable sexual relations between a man and a woman. She seemed to delight especially in describing the female orgasm, which she wrote was "a sense of heat in her brain," "a sensual delight" the taste of which "summons forth the emission of the man's seed." Although we know nothing of her sexual experiences, it would not be surprising to learn Hildegard had some first-hand knowledge. Her third vision begins with a description that reads like a modern-day account of a UFO. This is a woman who transcended her own time.

Hildegard spawned imitators in the centuries that followed. Brigitte of Sweden, Mechthild of Magdeburg, and many other women took up their pens, encouraged by the example of the great Hildegard, to write of their own visions, musings, philosophies, and observations of the natural and supernatural world. As a result, women gradually became more powerful in the Church. It is not too much of a stretch to trace the roots of modern feminism back to Hildegard of Bingen.

I believe we should read the words of Hildegard of Bingen as she wrote them and believed them to be, that is, as the Word of God made manifest to her through a miracle beyond her or any human's understanding. If we do, it is conceivable that we might just see past the world of our senses and our scientific instruments into a spiritual world that holds at least a small portion of our Maker's mind.

—HOMER HICKAM

SCIVIAS

These Are True Visions Flowing from God

And behold! In the forty-third year of my earthly course, as I was gazing with great fear and trembling attention at a heavenly vision, I saw a great splendor in which resounded a voice from Heaven, saying to me:

"O fragile human, ashes of ashes and filth of filth! Say and write what you see and hear. But since you are timid in speaking, simple in expounding, and untaught in writing, speak and write these things not by a human mouth, not by the understanding of human invention, and not by the requirements of human composition, but as you see and hear them on high in the heavenly places in the wonders of God. Explain these things in such a way that the hearer, receiving the words of his instructor, may expound them in those words, according to that will, vision, and instruction. Thus therefore, O human, speak these things that you see and hear. And write them not by yourself or any other human being, but by the will of Him who knows, sees, and disposes all things in the secrets of His mysteries."

And again I heard the voice from Heaven saying to me, "Speak therefore of these wonders and, being so taught, write them and speak."

It happened that, in the eleven hundred and forty-first year of the Incarnation of the Son of God, Jesus Christ, when I was forty-two years and seven months old, Heaven was opened and a fiery light of exceeding brilliance came and permeated my whole brain and inflamed my whole heart and my whole breast, not like a burning but like a warming flame, as the sun warms anything its rays touch. And immediately I knew the meaning of the exposition of the Scriptures, namely, the Psalter, the Gospel, and the other catholic volumes of both the Old and the New Testaments, though I did not have the interpretation of the words of their texts or the division of the syllables or the knowledge of cases or tenses. But I had sensed in myself wonderfully the power and mystery of secret and admirable visions from my childhood— that is, from the age of five—up to that time, as I do now. This, however, I showed to no one except a few religious persons who were living in the same manner as I; but meanwhile, until the time when God by His grace wished it to be manifested, I concealed it in quiet silence. But the visions I saw I did not perceive in dreams, sleep, or delirium, or by the eyes of the body, or by the ears of the outer self, or in hidden places; but I received them while awake and seeing with a pure mind and the eyes and ears of the inner self, in open places, as God willed it. How this might be is hard for mortal flesh to understand.

But when I had passed out of childhood and had reached the age of full maturity mentioned above, I heard a voice from Heaven saying, "I am the Living Light, who illuminates the darkness. The person [Hildegard] whom I have chosen and whom I have miraculously stricken as I willed, I have placed among great wonders, beyond the measure of the ancient people who saw in Me many secrets; but I have laid her low on the earth, that she might not set herself up in arrogance of mind. The world has had in her no joy or lewdness or use in worldly things, for I have withdrawn her from impudent boldness, and she feels fear and is timid in her works. For she suffers in her inmost being and in the veins of her flesh; she is distressed in mind and sense and endures great pain of body, because no security has dwelt in her, but in all her undertakings she has judged herself guilty. For I have closed up the cracks in her heart that her mind may not exalt itself in pride or vainglory, but may feel fear and grief rather than joy and wantonness. Hence, in My love she searched in her mind as to where she could find someone who would run in the path of salvation. And she found such a one and loved him [the monk Volmar of Disibodenberg], knowing that he was a faithful man, working like herself on another part of the work that leads to Me. And, holding fast to him, she worked with him in great zeal so that My hidden miracles might be revealed. And she did not seek to exalt herself above herself, but with many sighs bowed to him whom she found in the ascent of humility and the intention of good will.

"O human, who receives these things meant to manifest what is hidden not in the disquiet of deception but in the purity of simplicity, write, therefore, the things you see and hear."

But I, though I saw and heard these things, refused to write for a long time through doubt, bad opinion, and the diversity of human words, not with stubbornness but in the exercise of humility, until, laid low by the scourge of God, I fell upon a bed of sickness; then, compelled at last by many illnesses and by the witness of a certain noble maiden of good conduct [the nun Richardis of Stade] and of that man whom I had secretly sought and found, as mentioned above, I set my hand to the writing. While I was doing it, I sensed, as I mentioned before, the deep profundity of scriptural exposition; and, raising myself from illness by the strength I received, I brought this work to a close—though just barely—in ten years.

These visions took place and these words were written in the days of Henry, Archbishop of Mainz, and of Conrad, King of the Romans, and of Cuno, Abbot of Disibodenberg, under Pope Eugenius.

And I spoke and wrote these things not by the invention of my heart or that of any other person, but as by the secret mysteries of God I heard and received them in the heavenly places.

And again I heard a voice from Heaven saying to me, "Cry out, therefore, and write thus!"

BOOK ONE:

The Creator
and Creation

God Enthroned Shows Himself to Hildegard

I saw a great mountain the color of iron, and enthroned on it One of such great glory that it blinded my sight. On each side of Him there extended a soft shadow, like a wing of wondrous breadth and length. Before Him, at the foot of the mountain, stood an image full of eyes on all sides, in which, because of those eyes, I could discern no human form. In front of this image stood another, a child wearing a tunic of subdued color but white shoes, upon whose head such glory descended from the One enthroned upon that mountain that I could not look at its face. But from the One who sat enthroned upon that mountain many living sparks sprang forth, which flew very sweetly around the images. Also, I perceived in this mountain many little windows, in which appeared human heads, some of subdued colors and some white.

And behold, He who was enthroned upon that mountain cried out in a strong, loud voice saying, "O human, who are fragile dust of the earth and ashes of ashes! Cry out and speak of the origin of pure salvation until those people are instructed, who, though they see the inmost contents of the Scriptures, do not wish to tell them or preach them, because they are lukewarm and sluggish in serving God's justice. Unlock for them the enclosure of mysteries that they, timid as they are, conceal in a hidden and fruitless field. Burst forth into a fountain of abundance and overflow with mystical knowledge, until they who now think you contemptible because of Eve's transgression are stirred up by the flood of your irrigation. For you have received your irrigation. For you have received your profound insight not from humans, but from the lofty and tremendous Judge on high, where this calmness will shine strongly with glorious light among the shining ones.

"Arise, therefore, cry out and tell what is shown to you by the strong power of God's help, for He who rules every creature in might and kindness floods those who fear Him and serve Him in sweet love and humility with the glory of heavenly enlightenment and leads those who persevere in the way of justice to the joys of the Eternal Vision."

The strength and stability of God's eternal kingdom

As you see, therefore, *the great mountain the color of iron*[1] symbolizes the strength and stability of the eternal Kingdom of God, which no fluctuation of mutability can destroy; and *the One enthroned upon it of such great glory that it blinds your sight* is the One in the Kingdom of Beatitude who rules the whole world with celestial divinity in the brilliance of unfading serenity, but is incomprehensible to human minds. But that *on each side of Him there extends a soft shadow like a wing of wonderful breadth and length* shows that both in admonition and in punishment ineffable justice displays sweet and gentle protection and perseveres in true equity.

Concerning fear of the Lord

And before Him at the foot of the mountain stands an image full of eyes on all sides. For the Fear of the Lord stands in God's presence with humility and gazes on the Kingdom of God, surrounded by the

---

[1]Italics indicate portions of the initial vision that are repeated and explained in the interpretation, which follows.

clarity of a good and just intention, exercising her zeal and stability among humans. And thus *you can discern no human form in her on account of those eyes.* For by the acute sight of her contemplation she counters all forgetfulness of God's justice, which people often feel in their mental tedium, so no inquiry by weak mortals eludes her vigilance.

Concerning those who are poor in spirit

And so *before this image appears another image, that of a child wearing a tunic of subdued color but white shoes.* For when the Fear of the Lord leads, they who are poor in spirit follow; for the Fear of the Lord holds fast in humble devotion to the blessedness of poverty of spirit, which does not seek boasting or elation of heart, but loves simplicity and sobriety of mind, attributing its just works not to itself but to God in pale subjection, wearing, as it were, a tunic of subdued color and faithfully following the serene footsteps of the Son of God. *Upon her head descends such glory from the One enthroned upon that mountain that you cannot look at her face;* because He who rules every created being imparts the power and strength of this blessedness by the great clarity of His visitation, and weak, mortal thought cannot grasp His purpose, since He who possesses celestial riches submitted Himself humbly to poverty.

They who fear God and love poverty of spirit are the guardians of virtues

But from the One who is enthroned upon that mountain many living sparks go forth, which fly about those images with great sweetness. This means that many exceedingly strong virtues come forth from Almighty God, darting fire in divine glory; these ardently embrace and captivate those who truly fear God and who faithfully love poverty of spirit, surrounding them with their help and protection.

The aims of human acts cannot be hidden from God's knowledge

Wherefore in this mountain you see many little windows, in which appear human heads, some of subdued color and some white. For in the most high, profound, and perspicuous knowledge of God the aims of human acts cannot be concealed or hidden. Most often they display both lukewarmness and purity, since people now slumber in guilt, weary in their hearts and in their deeds, and now awaken and keep watch in honor. Solomon bears witness to this for Me, saying:

Solomon on this subject

"The slothful hand has brought about poverty, but the hand of the industrious man prepares riches" [Prov. 10:4]; which means a person makes himself weak and poor when he will not work justice, avoid wickedness, or pay a debt, remaining idle in the face of the wonders of the works of beatitude. But one who does strong works of salvation, running in the way of truth, obtains the upwelling fountain of glory, by which he prepares himself most precious riches on earth and in Heaven.

Therefore whoever has knowledge in the Holy Spirit and wings of faith, let this one not ignore My admonition, but taste it, embrace it, and receive it in his soul.

The Universe and Its Symbolism

After this I saw a vast instrument, round and shadowed, in the shape of an egg, small at the top, large in the middle, and narrowed at the bottom; outside it, surrounding its circumference, there was bright fire with, as it were, a shadowy zone under it. And in that fire there was a globe of sparkling flame so great that the whole instrument was illuminated by it, over which three little torches were arranged in such a way that by their fire they held up the globe lest it fall. And that globe at times raised itself up, so that much fire flew to it and thereby its flames lasted longer; and sometimes it sank downward and great cold came to it, so that its flames were more quickly subdued.

But from the fire that surrounded the instrument issued a blast with whirl-winds, and from the zone beneath it rushed forth another blast with its own whirlwinds, which diffused themselves hither and thither throughout the instrument. In that zone too there was a dark fire of such great horror that I could not look at it, whose force shook the whole zone, full of thunder, tempest, and exceedingly sharp stones both large and small. And while it made its thunders heard, the bright fire and the winds and the air were in commotion, so that lightning preceded those thunders; for the fire felt within itself the turbulence of the thunder.

But beneath that zone was purest ether, with no zone beneath it, and in it I saw a globe of white fire and great magnitude over which two little torches were placed, holding that globe so that it would not exceed the measure of its course. And in that ether were scattered many bright spheres, into which the white globe from time to time poured itself out and emitted its brightness, and then moved back under the globe of red fire and renewed its flames from it, and then again sent them out into those spheres. And from that ether too a blast came forth with its whirlwinds, which spread itself everywhere throughout the instrument.

And beneath that ether I saw watery air with a white zone beneath it, which diffused itself here and there and imparted moisture to the whole instrument. And when it suddenly contracted, it sent forth sudden rain with great noise, and when it gently spread out, it gave a pleasant and softly falling rain. But from it too came a blast with its whirlwinds, which spread itself throughout the aforementioned instrument.

And in the midst of these elements was a sandy globe of great magnitude, which these elements had so surrounded that it could not waver in any direction. But as these elements and these blasts contended with each other, by their strength they made it move a little.

And I saw between the north and the east a great mountain, which to the north had great darkness and to the east had great light, but in such a way that the light could not reach the darkness, nor the darkness the light.

And again I heard the voice from Heaven saying to me:

The visible and temporal are a manifestation of the invisible and eternal

God, who made all things by His will, created them so that His Name would be known and glorified, showing in them not just the things that are visible and temporal, but also the things that are invisible and eternal. Which is demonstrated by this vision you are perceiving.

The firmament in the likeness of an egg and what it signifies

For this vast instrument, round and shadowy, in the shape of an egg, small at the top, large in the middle, and narrowed at the bottom, faithfully shows Omnipotent God, incomprehensible in His majesty and inestimable in His mysteries and the hope of all the faithful; for humanity at first was rude and rough and simple in its actions, but later was enlarged through the Old and New Testaments, and finally at the end of the world is destined to be beset with many tribulations.

On the bright fire and the shadowy zone

Outside it, surrounding its circumference, there is bright fire with, as it were, a shadowy zone under it. This shows that God consumes by the fire of His vengeance all those who are outside the true faith, and those who remain within the Catholic faith He purifies by the fire of His consolation; thus He throws down the darkness of devilish perversity, as He did also when the Devil wanted to oppose himself to God, though God had created him, and so fell defeated into perdition.

On the placement of the sun and the three stars

And in that fire there is a globe of sparkling flame, so great that the whole instrument is illuminated by it, which in the splendor of its brightness shows that within God the Father is His ineffable Only-Begotten, the Sun of Justice with the brilliance of burning charity, of such great glory that every creature is illumined by the brightness of

His light. *Over this three little torches are arranged in such a way that by their fire they hold up the globe lest it fall;* that is, [the Trinity] shows how by its arrangement the Son of God, leaving the angels in the heavenly places, descended to earth and showed humans, who exist in soul and body, heavenly things, so that, glorifying Him by serving Him, they reject all harmful error and magnify Him as the true Son of God incarnate through the true Virgin, when the angel foretold Him and when humans, living in soul and body, with faithful joy received Him.

On the ascent of the sun and what it signifies

Therefore *the globe sometimes raises itself up, so that much fire flies to it and therefore its flames last longer.* This means that when the time came that the Only-Begotten of God was to become incarnate for the redemption and uplifting of the human race by the will of the Father, the Holy Spirit by the power of the Father brought celestial mysteries wonderfully to pass in the Blessed Virgin; so that when the Son of God too in virginal chastity showed marvelous splendor and made virginity fruitful, virginity became glorious, for the longed-for Incarnation was brought to pass in the noble Virgin.

On the descent of the sun and what it signifies

So, indeed, *sometimes it sinks downward and great cold comes to it, so that its flames are more quickly subdued.* This shows that the Only-Begotten of God, born of a virgin and hence inclined to be merciful to human poverty, incurred many miseries and sustained great physical anguish; but after He had shown Himself to the world in a bodily shape, He passed from the world and returned to the Father, while His disciples stood by, as it is written:

Words from the Acts of the Apostles

"While they looked on He was lifted up, and a cloud received Him" [Acts 1:9]. Which is to say: When the children of the Church had received the Son of God in the interior knowledge of their hearts, the sanctity of His body was lifted up into the power of His Divinity, and in a mystical miracle the cloud of secret mystery received Him, hiding Him from mortal eyes, and the blasts of the winds showed themselves His servants.

On the first wind and its whirlwinds

But, as you see, from the fire that surrounds the instrument issues a blast with whirlwinds, which shows that from Almighty God, who fills the whole world with His power, truth rushes forth and spreads with words of justice, which truly demonstrate to humanity the same living and true God.

On the second wind and its whirlwinds

But from the zone beneath it rushes forth another blast with its own whirlwinds, because the rage of the Devil, knowing God and fearing Him, sends out the worst dishonor and the most evil utterances, which diffuse themselves hither and thither throughout the instrument, since in the world useful and useless rumors spread themselves abroad in many ways among the peoples.

On the dark fire, the thunder, and the sharp stones

In this zone also there is a dark fire of such horror that you cannot look at it. This means that the ancient betrayer's most evil and most vile snares vomit forth blackest murder with such great passion that the human intellect cannot fathom its insanity; whose force shakes the whole zone, because murder includes in its horror all diabolical malignities. In the first man born hatred boiled up out of anger and led to fratricide, full of thunder, tempest, and exceedingly sharp stones large and small, for murder is full of avarice, drunkenness, and extreme hardness of heart, which run riot relentlessly both in great murders and in minor vices. While it makes its thunders heard, the bright fire and the winds and the air are all in commotion, because when murder cries out in its eagerness to shed blood, it arouses the justice of Heaven and an outburst of flying rumors and an increased disposition to vengeance on the part of right judgment; so that lightning precedes those thunders, for the fire feels in itself the turbulence of the thunder, for the manifestation of divine scrutiny exceeds and suppresses evil, since the Divine Majesty, before the sound of that insanity manifests itself in public, foresees it with that watchful eye to which all things are naked.

The purest ether and the placement of the moon and two stars

But beneath that zone is purest ether, with no zone beneath it; for beneath the snares of the ancient betrayer shines most serene faith, with no uncertainty or infidelity hiding in it, since it is not founded by itself but dependent on Christ; and in it you see a globe of white fire *and great magnitude,* which is a true symbol of the unconquered Church, which, as you can see, asserts in faith innocent brightness and great honor. *Over this two little torches are placed, holding that globe so that it does not exceed the measure of its course,* which signifies that the two Testaments given from Heaven, the Old and the New, connect it to the divine rules of the celestial mysteries, holding the Church back from rushing into a variety of different practices, for both the Old and the New Testaments show it the blessedness of the supernal heritage.

The placement of the other stars and what it signifies

And therefore *in that ether are scattered many bright spheres, into which the white globe from time to time pours itself out and emits its brightness;* for in the purity of faith many splendid works of piety are done by which the Church, though it may suffer words of disdain, passes on the beauty of its miracles. Though plunged in sorrow, it still marvels at the brightness of the works done by the perfected through others; and therefore it *moves back under the globe of red fire and renews its flames from it, and then again sends them out into those spheres;* for, moving in contrition back under the protection of the Only-Begotten of God and receiving from Him the pardon of divine consolation, it again shows the love of heavenly things in blessed works.

The third wind and its whirlwinds and what they signify

Therefore also *from the ether a blast comes forth with its whirlwinds, which spreads itself everywhere throughout the instrument;* for from the unity of faith there comes forth to help humanity a strong tradition of true and perfect statements, which swiftly penetrate to the ends of the earth.

The watery air and the white zone and what they signify

And beneath that ether you see watery air with a white zone beneath it, which diffuses itself here and there and imparts moisture to the whole instrument; for thus, under the faith possessed by the ancient and the modern fathers, baptism in the Church for the salvation of believers is truly shown to you, which, founded on blessed innocence and stability, propagates itself everywhere by divine inspiration and brings to the whole world the overflowing waters of salvation for believers. *When this zone suddenly contracts, it sends forth sudden rain with great noise, and when it gently spreads out, it gives a pleasant and softly falling rain;* for sometimes baptism is presented by the apostles of truth with all their enthusiasm of preaching and depth of mind, and so manifests itself to the astonishment of humans with a rapid abundance of words and a flood of preaching; and sometimes that same baptism is presented by those preachers with sweet moderation, so that it reaches the people for whom it is meant discreetly by a gentle watering.

On the fourth wind and its whirlwinds

Therefore from that air too comes a blast with its whirlwinds that spreads itself throughout the aforementioned instrument; for when the flood of baptism brings salvation to believers, a true report of the words of forcible sermons goes forth and pervades the whole world with its manifest blessedness, so that the people, forsaking infidelity and seeking after the Catholic faith, openly declare it.

On the sandy globe of the earth and what it signifies

And in the midst of these elements is a sandy globe of great magnitude, which these elements have so surrounded that it cannot waver in any direction. This openly shows that, of all the strengths of God's creation, Man's is most profound, made in a wondrous way with great glory from the dust of the earth and so entangled with the strengths of the rest of creation that he can never be separated from them; for the elements of the world, created for Man's service, wait on him, and Man, enthroned as it were in their midst, by divine disposition presides over them, as David says, inspired by Me:

Words of David on this subject

"Thou hast crowned him with glory and worship, and given him dominion over all the works of Thy hands" [Ps. 8:5–6]. Which is to say: You, O God, who have marvelously made all things, have crowned Man with the gold and purple crown of intellect and with the sublime garment of visible beauty, thus placing him like a prince above the height of Your perfect works, which You have distributed justly and rightly among Your creatures. Before all Your other creatures You have conferred on Man great and wonderful dignities.

On the movement of the earth and what it signifies

But, as you see, *as these elements and these blasts contend with each other, by their strength they make the globe move a little;* for at certain times the report of the Creator's miracles comes to all of God's creation, so that miracle is piled on miracle in a great thunder of words; and then Man, struck by the greatness of these miracles, feels the impact on his mind and body and in these wondrous deeds considers with astonishment his own weakness and frailty.

The great mountain between the north and the east

And you see between the north and the east a great mountain, which to the north has great darkness and to the east has great light. This shows Man's great choice between devilish impiety and divine goodness, evil deception giving the many miseries of damnation to the reprobate, and salvation giving the great happiness of redemption to the elect; *but in such a way that the light cannot reach the darkness, nor the darkness the light;* for the works of light do not come down among the works of darkness, and the works of darkness do not ascend to the works of light, though the Devil often tries to obscure the latter through evil people, like pagans, heretics, and false prophets and those whom they try to attract to themselves by fallacious deception. How? Because they want to know what it is not for them to know, imitating the one who panted to be like the Most High. And because they follow him, by their own will he shows them a lie as the truth. Hence they are not with Me, and I am not with them; for they do not walk in My ways, but love strange paths, seeking out the false things a foolish creature shows them about future events. And in their perverse seeking this is what they wish to have, despising Me and rejecting My saints, who love Me with a sincere heart.

Those who perversely examine the future by means of creatures

But these people who obstinately tempt Me by perverse art, examining creatures that were made for their service and asking them to show them things their willfulness wishes to know—can they, by practicing this art, lengthen or shorten the time their Creator has given them to live? They cannot, by a day or by an hour. Or can they postpone what God has predetermined? In no way. O wretches! Do I not sometimes permit creatures to show you what will happen? They can show you these signs because they fear Me, God, as a servant can sometimes display the power of his master, and as the ox, the ass, and other animals show the will of their masters when they faithfully do their bidding. O fools! When you consign Me to forgetfulness, neither looking to Me nor adoring Me, but looking to a creature subject to you for what it portends and shows, then you are obstinately casting Me aside, worshiping the frail creature instead of your Creator. Therefore I say to you: O human, why do you worship that creature, which cannot console you or help you and which cannot make you prosper in happiness, though it is affirmed that they can by astrologers, teachers of death, and followers of pagan unbelief, who say the stars give life to you humans and determine all your actions? O wretches, who made the stars? But at times, with My permission, the stars by certain signs do manifest themselves to humanity, as My Son shows in His Gospel, where He says:

Words of the Gospel

"There shall be signs in the sun and the moon and the stars" [Luke 21:25]. Which is to say: By the light of these lights service is rendered to humanity, and in their revolutions the times of times are displayed. So in the latest times, by My permission lamentable and dangerous epochs will be foretold in them, so that the radiance of the sun, the splendor of the moon, and the brightness of the stars will be dimmed, that human hearts may be stirred up to action. Thus also by My will the Incarnation of My Son was shown by a star. But no human being has a star of his own, which determines his life, as a foolish and erring people tries to assert; all stars are at the service of all people. That star only shone more brightly than all other stars because My Only-Begotten, unlike all other humans, was born without sin from a virgin birth. But that star gave My Son no aid, except in faithfully announcing His Incarnation to the people; for all stars and other creatures, fearing Me, fulfill My command, but do not have any knowledge of anything about any creature. For creatures fulfill My commands when it pleases Me, in the same way as when a minter, making a coin, strikes it with the requisite form; then that coin displays the form stamped on it, but has no power to know when the minter may decide to impress another form on it, for neither in the long nor in the short run does it understand the form it has. What does this mean?

O human, if a stone lay before you on which, if you looked carefully, you could read what was going to happen to you, then in your mistaken thoughts, saddened by your misfortune or elated by your prosperity, you would say, "Alas, I shall die!" or "O joy, I shall live!" or "Alas, what misfortune!" or "O joy, what prosperity is mine!" Now what would that stone have conferred on you? Would it have taken away or given you anything? It could not be either against you or for you.

And likewise neither stars nor fire nor birds nor any other creatures of this kind can either harm you or help you by your examining them. But if, rejecting Me, you trust in a creature made for your service, I also in My just judgment will cast you out of My sight, taking from you the felicity of My Kingdom. For I do not want you to scrutinize stars or fire or birds or other creatures for signs of future events; and if you persist in scrutinizing them, your eyes are obnoxious to Me, and I will cast you out like the lost angel, who deserted the truth and threw himself into damnation.

O human! When the stars and the other creatures were made, where were you? Did you give God advice about their arrangement? But the presumption of such scrutiny arose in the first of all dissensions, when Man forgot God to such an extent that he arrogantly inspected one kind of creature after another and sought in them signs of future events. And thus, indeed, the error arose about Baal, because people who were deceived worshiped the creature of God instead of God, to which the Devil's mockery incited them, because they were mindful of the creature rather than the Creator and desired to know what they were not meant to know.

How the Devil mocks humanity by the art of magic

Therefore worse things than this appeared, for humans through the Devil began to be crazy for magic arts, so that now they see and hear the Devil, and he speaks to them deceitfully and shows them one sort of creature in their scrutiny as if it were another. It is not My will to say how the first seducers were taught by the Devil, so that now those who seek him see and hear him; but they are very guilty in this wickedness of theirs, for they deny Me, their God, and imitate the ancient seducer. O human! I have sought you by the blood of My Son, not in malicious iniquity but in great justice; but you forsake Me, the true God, and imitate him who is a liar. I am justice and truth; and therefore I admonish you by faith, exhort you by love, and recapture you by penitence, so that, though you are bloody in the pollutions of sinners, you may yet rise from your fall into ruin. But if you despise Me, understand the comparison in this parable, which says:

A parable on this subject

A certain lord who had many servants under him gave each of them a full set of warlike arms, saying, "Be upright and useful, and renounce tardiness and indolence." But while they were marching with him, these servants saw beside the road a certain impostor, inventor of evil arts; and some of them, being deceived, said, "We wish to learn this man's arts!" And, casting away their arms, they ran to him. The others said to them, "What are you doing, imitating this impostor and provoking our lord to anger?" And they answered, "How does this harm our lord?" But their lord said to them, "O wicked servants! Why have you thrown away the arms I gave you? And why is it dearer to you to love this vanity than to serve me, your lord, whose servants you are? Go, then, follow this impostor as you desire, for you do not wish to serve me, and see how his folly will profit you." And he cast them out. Which is to say:

This lord is Almighty God, ruling all peoples with His power, who has armed every person with intellect, commanding him to be active and vigilant in the exercise of virtue and rid himself of perverseness and negligence. But as people are going along the way of truth, disposed to walk in the divine commands, they are met by many temptations; for the Devil, the seducer of the whole world and the wicked contriver of many vices, waits for them not in the way of truth, but in deceptive ambushes. Therefore certain of them who love injustice more than right are seduced by the Devil and are more eager to imitate the vices of the ancient seducer than to embrace the virtues of God. And that intellect, which they ought to have used for the divine commandments, they twist to the vices of earthly iniquity and submit themselves to the Devil.

The doctors, as their companions, cite to them often the sacred Scriptures, reproaching them for their deeds and loudly asking why they follow the Devil's illusions and bring down divine vengeance on themselves. But they almost always deride these admonitions, claiming that they sin in few things and do not offend God by pride at all. Therefore when they persevere in that obduracy, they receive the divine sentence; for these servants of iniquity are asked why they suffocated their God-given intellect and why they preferred the deceptions of the ancient seducer to loving their Creator, whom they should actively have served. Thus they too are despised for devilish illusions according to their works, since they refused to serve God, and they are forced to consider what their wicked seduction has profited them, since, thus cast out, they incur damnation because they have disregarded the divine precepts and tried to follow the Devil rather than God.

For I do not will that humans should despise Me, when they ought to know Me in faith; for if they reject Me to examine a creature subject to them, thus imitating the ancient seducer, then I permit them to achieve the desires of their hearts both as to the creature and as to the Devil; and thus they learn by experience how much the creature they have adored will profit them and what the Devil whom they have followed will give them.

Humans go out of the world whenever their salvation and use is complete

And, O foolish humans, why do you scrutinize a creature about the length of your life? For none of you can either know or avoid or get through the period of his life except as I decide he will live; for, O human, when your salvation is complete in both worldly and spiritual matters, you will leave the present world and pass on to that which has no end. For when a person has such fortitude that he burns for Me more ardently than other people and, aware of the earthly dregs of stinking sin, is active in avoiding the snares of the ancient serpent, I do not take his spirit from his body before his fruits have fully ripened with sweetest fragrance. But if I find one who is of such frailty that in pain of his body and terror of the evil lurker he is too delicate to bear My yoke, I take him away from this world before his soul, wasting away in weakness, begins to dry up. For I know all things. But I want to caution the human race with all possible justice, so that no person can excuse himself: When I strike them with a sentence of death as if they were about to die, when in fact they are to live for a long time yet, I warn and exhort people to do justice. For no one can have or make for himself any time unless I see usefulness in him and by My will allow him to live; as indeed Job testifies, when he says:

Words of Job on this subject

"You have appointed his bounds, which cannot be passed" [Job 14:5]. Which is to say: You who are above all and foresee all before it comes to pass have indeed established in the secret of Your majesty the bounds of human life, so that they cannot be exceeded by humans either by knowledge, prudence, understanding, or for any reason, in infancy, youth, or old age, except according to Your secret providence, which willed to make Man for the glory of Your Name.

Words of God on this subject

I, O human, knew you before the foundation of the world. Nevertheless, I will to consider your days in your works and judge of their usefulness and diligently and sharply examine your deeds. But if I suddenly withdraw anyone from this life, the usefulness of his life is complete; and if his life were extended longer, it would not keep on in freshness bearing good fruits but, tainted by the faith of the flesh, would only give off smoke like the empty sound of words and not attain to Me in the inmost depth of its heart. Therefore I do not grant him a prolongation of this life, but withdraw him from this world before he falls into the apathy of this infertility. But to you, O human, I say: Why do you despise Me? Did I not send My prophets to you, give My Son on the wood of the cross for your salvation, and choose My apostles to show you the way of truth through the Gospel? So, having all good things through Me, you cannot excuse yourself. And why then do you put Me off?

God will no longer tolerate auguries from creatures

But I will no longer tolerate this perverse error, your seeking signs for your actions in the stars, fire, birds, or any other creatures; all those who by the Devil's persuasion first fell into this error despised God and threw down His precepts, for which they themselves are despised. But I shine above every creature in the glory of My Divinity, and My miracles are manifested to you in My saints; so I wish you not to practice this error of augury anymore, but to look toward Me.

Concerning human foolishness and stubbornness

O fool! Who am I? None other than the Supreme Good. Therefore I grant you all good things when you diligently seek Me.
And whom do you believe Me to be? I am God, above all things
and in all things, but you want to treat Me as a serf who fears his
lord. How? You want Me to do your will, while you despise My
precepts. God is not thus. What does this mean? He does not
remember a beginning or fear an end. The heavens contemplate
Me, resound with My praises, and obey Me in that justice by
which I established them. The sun, moon, and stars appear
among the clouds of Heaven on their proper course, and the
blasts of the wind and the rain move through the air as is
appointed for them, and all do the bidding of their Creator. But
you, O human, do not fulfill My precepts, but follow your own
will, as if for you the law's justice were neither established nor
manifested. And although you are but ashes, you are in such a
state of contumacy that the justice of My law does not suffice for
you, though it is plowed and cultivated in the body and blood of
My Son and well trodden out by My saints of the Old and New
Testaments alike.

Analogy of the goat, the hart, and the wolf

But in your great foolishness you wish to lay hold of Me, threat-
ening Me and saying, "If God wants me to be just and good,
why does He not make me righteous?" Wishing to catch Me like
this is as if a wanton goat wished to catch a hart; it would be
thrown back and pierced by the hart's strong horns. So, when

you try to behave wantonly and play with Me, I too will crush you in My just judgment by the precepts of the law as if by My horns. These trumpets resound in your ears, but you do not follow them; you run off after the wolf, which you think you have so mastered that it cannot hurt you. But the wolf will devour you, saying, "This sheep strayed from the road and did not want to follow its shepherd but ran after me; therefore I will to have it, for it chose me and forsook its shepherd." O human, God is just; so everything He does in Heaven and earth is justly ordained.

Analogy of the physician

I am the great Physician of all diseases and act like a doctor who sees a sick man who longs to be cured. What does this mean? If the illness is slight, he cures it easily, but if it is serious, he says to the sick person, "I require silver and gold from you. If you will give them to me, I will help you." I too, O human, do this. Lesser sins I wipe away in people's groans and tears and good resolutions, but for graver faults I say, O human, apply yourself to penitence and amendment, and I will show you My mercy and give you eternal life. You shall not scrutinize the stars and other creatures about future events, adore the Devil, or invoke him or ask him anything. For if you seek to know more than you ought to know, you will be deceived by the ancient seducer. The first man sought more than he should have sought and was deceived by him and went to perdition. But the Devil did not foresee the redemption of Man, when the Son of Man slew death and broke

Hell asunder. The Devil at first conquered Man through the woman; but God at last crushed the Devil through the woman who bore the Son of God, who wondrously brought the works of the Devil to naught, as My beloved John testifies, saying:

Words of John

"For this reason the Son of God appeared, that He might destroy the works of the Devil" [1 John 3:8]. What does this mean? The great brightness, the Son of God, appeared for the health and salvation of humanity, taking on the poverty of a human body, but shining like a burning star amid shadowy clouds. He was placed on the winepress, where wine was to be pressed out without the dregs of fermentation, because He, the Cornerstone, fell upon the press and made such wine that it gave forth the greatest odor of sweetness. He, shining as a glorious human being amid the human race, without any admixture of polluted blood, trod with His warlike foot upon the head of the ancient serpent; He destroyed all the darts of his iniquity, full of rage and lust as they were, and made him utterly contemptible.

Therefore whoever has knowledge in the Holy Spirit and wings of faith, let this one not ignore My admonition, but taste it, embrace it, and receive it in his soul.

The Synagogue

After this, I saw the image of a woman, pale from her head to her navel and black from her navel to her feet; her feet were red, and around her feet was a cloud of purest whiteness. She had no eyes, and had put her hands in her armpits; she stood next to the altar that is before the eyes of God, but she did not touch it. And in her heart stood Abraham, and in her breast Moses, and in her womb the rest of the prophets, each displaying his symbols and admiring the beauty of the Church. She was of great size, like the tower of a city, and had on her head a circlet like the dawn.

And again I heard the voice from Heaven saying to me: "On the people of the Old Testament God placed the austerity of the Law in enjoining circumcision on Abraham; which He then turned into sweet Grace when He gave His Son to those who believed in the truth of the Gospel, and anointed with the oil of mercy those who had been wounded by the yoke of the Law."

The Synagogue is the mother of the Incarnation of the Son of God

Therefore *you see the image of a woman, pale from her head to her navel;* she is the Synagogue, which is the mother of the Incarnation of the Son of God. From the time her children began to be born until their full strength she foresaw in the shadows the secrets of God, but did not fully reveal them. For she was not the glowing dawn who speaks openly, but gazed on the latter from afar with great admiration and alluded to her thus in the Song of Songs:

Words of Solomon

"Who is this who comes up from the desert, flowing with delights and leaning upon her beloved?" [Song of Sol. 3:6; 8:5]. Which is to say: Who is this new Bride, who with many good works comes up through the deserts of the pagans, who reject God's lawful precepts and adore idols, and ascends to heavenly desires, abounding in the delights of the gifts of the Holy Spirit, panting with great zeal and leaning on her spouse, the Son of God? For it is she who blooms with the resplendent virtues given her by the Son of God and flows with brooks of Scripture. And the same Synagogue, lost in admiration of the children of this new Bride, speaks thus by My servant the prophet Isaiah:

Words of Isaiah the prophet

"Who are these who fly like clouds, and like doves to their windows?" [Isa. 60:8]. That is to say: Who are these who, withdrawing themselves in mind from earthly and fleshly desires, fly full of desire and devotion to heavenly things, and with the simplicity of doves and without the bitterness of gall fortify their senses, and with the great ardor of virtue seek the protection of that firm rock that is the Only-Begotten of God? For these are they who in supernal love tread underfoot earthly kingdoms and seek heavenly ones. The Synagogue, therefore, was marveling at the Church, for she knew herself not to be adorned with those virtues she foresaw in her; for the Church is surrounded by angelic guardians to keep the Devil from harming her and casting her down, while the Synagogue, deserted by God, lies in vice.

On the varying color of the Synagogue

That is why *you see her black from her navel to her feet,* for from the time of her fullest strength to the end of her time she was soiled by deviation from the Law and by transgression of the heritage of her fathers, for she disregarded the divine precepts in many ways and followed the pleasures of the flesh. *Her feet are red, and around her feet is a cloud of purest whiteness,* for at the end of her time she killed the Prophet of Prophets and therefore slipped and fell down herself; while at the same time a most clear and acute faith arose in the minds of believers, for as the Synagogue ended, the Church arose, when after the death of the Son of God the apostolic doctrine spread throughout the world.

Her blindness, and why the prophets stand within her

That image *has no eyes, and has put her hands in her armpits;* for the Synagogue did not look on the true light, since she held the Only-Begotten of God in despite, and she conceals the works of justice under the apathy of her laziness, remaining in her torpor and negligently hiding them as if they did not exist. *She stands next to the altar that is before the eyes of God, but she does not touch it;* for she did in fact know superficially the Law of God, which she received by divine precept and divine visitation, but she did not plumb its depths, for she shrank from it rather than loved it, neglecting the sacrifice and the incense of devout prayers to God.

And in her heart stands Abraham, for he was the beginning of circumcision in the Synagogue; *and in her breast Moses,* for he brought the divine Law into human hearts; *and in her womb the rest of the prophets,* for they stand in that tradition that was given them by God as observers of the divine precepts; *each displaying his symbols and admiring the beauty of the Church,* for they displayed the miracles of their prophecies by marvelous symbols and with great wonder waited for the noble beauty of the new Bride.

That she is as great as a tower and has a circlet like the dawn

The Synagogue is of great size like the tower of a city, because she received the greatness of the divine laws and so foreshadowed the bulwarks and defenses of the noble and chosen City. *And she has on her head a circlet like the dawn,* because she prefigured in her rising the miracle of God's Only-Begotten and foreshadowed the bright virtues and mysteries that followed. For she was crowned, as it were, early in the morning, when she received the divine precepts, following Adam, who at first accepted God's commands, but afterward by his transgressions fell into death. So also did the Jews, who originally submitted to the divine Law, but then in their unbelief rejected the Son of God. But as humanity in the last days will be snatched from the perdition of death by the death of God's Only-Begotten, so too the Synagogue, stirred up by divine clemency, will before the last day abandon her unbelief and truly attain to the knowledge of God.

How is this? Does not the dawn rise before the sun? But the dawn recedes, and the sun's brightness remains. How is this? The Old Testament receded, and the truth of the Gospel remains; for what the early people observed in the flesh in legal rites the new people of the New Testament practice in the spirit, and what the former showed in the flesh the latter perfect in the spirit. For circumcision has not passed away, because it has been transformed into baptism; as the older race was marked in one member, the newer race is marked in all its members. Hence the old precepts have not passed away, but are transformed into better ones; and in the last times the Synagogue will also transform itself faithfully into the Church. For, O Synagogue, when you were wandering in many iniquities, polluting yourself with Baal and the others, shamefully breaking the custom of the Law and lying naked in your sins, I did what My servant Ezekiel tells of when he says:

Words of Ezekiel

"I spread my garment over you and covered your shame; and I swore to you, and I entered into a covenant with you" [Ezek. 16:8]. Which is to say: I, the Son of the Most High, in the will of My Father have spread My Incarnation over you, O Synagogue, to save you, taking away your sins, which you have committed in many times of forgetfulness; I have promised you the remedy of salvation, showing you the ways of My covenant for it when I made known to you by apostolic doctrine the true faith, so that you might obey my precepts as a wife ought to submit to the power of her husband. For I have taken from you the harshness of the exterior Law and given you the sweetness of spiritual doctrine and in it shown you all My mysteries in Myself; but you have deserted Me, who am just, and allied with the Devil.

Analogy of Samson, Saul, and David

But, O human, understand that Samson's wife left him, and so he was deprived of his eyesight, and the Synagogue likewise forsook the Son of God, spurning Him stubbornly and rejecting His doctrine. But later, when his hair grew again, as the Church of God was strengthened, the Son of God in His might overthrew the Synagogue and deprived her children, who were crushed by God's jealousy by means of pagans who did not know God. For she had undergone many errors of confusion and discord and polluted herself by wicked transgressions. But as David at last called back the wife he had first married, but who had polluted herself with another man, so also the Son of God at the end of time will call back the Synagogue, which had first been joined to Him in His Incarnation, but had rejected the grace of baptism and followed the Devil, and she will forsake the errors of unbelief and return to the light of truth. For the Devil drew the Synagogue away in her blindness and gave her over to error and unbelief; and he will not cease to do this until the coming of the son of perdition. But the latter will fall in the exaltation of his pride as Saul fell, slain on Mount Gilboa, after driving David out of his land, as the son of iniquity will try to drive out My Son in His elect.

But My Son, when the Antichrist has been cast out, will call back the Synagogue to the true faith, as David took back his first wife after the death of Saul; for at the end of time the people will see the one who deceived them conquered and run back with great haste to the way of salvation. For it was not fitting for the truth of the Gospel to precede the shadow of the Law, as it is fitting that fleshly things should precede and spiritual things should follow; the servant announces his master's coming, and the master does not go before the servant to serve him. So too the Synagogue went before as a foreshadowing sign, and the Church came after in the light of truth.

Therefore whoever has knowledge in the Holy Spirit and wings of faith, let this one not ignore My admonition, but taste it, embrace it, and receive it in his soul.

The Choirs of Angels

Then I saw in the secret places in the heights of Heaven two armies of heavenly spirits who shone with great brightness. Those in one of the armies had on their breasts wings, with forms like human forms in front of them, on which human features showed as if in clear water. Those in the second army also had wings on their breasts, which displayed forms like human forms, in which the image of the Son of Man shone as if in a mirror. And I could see no other form either in these or in the others. These armies were arrayed in the shape of a crown around five other armies.

Those in the first of these five armies seemed as if they had human forms that shone with great splendor from the shoulders down. Those in the second shone with such great brightness that I could not look at them. Those in the third had the appearance of white marble and heads like human heads, over which torches were burning, and from the shoulders down they were surrounded by an iron gray cloud. Those in the fourth had forms like human forms and feet like human feet, and wore helmets on their heads, and marble tunics. And those in the fifth had nothing human in their appearance, and shone red like the dawn. And I saw no other form in them.

But these armies were also arrayed like a crown around two others. Those in the first of these other armies seemed to be full of eyes and wings, and in each eye appeared a mirror and in each mirror a human form, and they raised their wings to a celestial height. And those in the second burned like fire and had many wings, in which they showed as if in a mirror all the Church ranks arrayed in order. And I saw no other shape either in these or in the others. And all these armies were

singing with marvelous voices all kinds of music about the wonders that God
works in blessed souls, and by this God was magnificently glorified.

And I heard the voice from Heaven saying to me:

God wonderfully formed and ordered His creation

Almighty and Ineffable God, who was before all ages and had no
beginning and will not cease to be when all ages are ended, marvelously by His will created every creature and marvelously by
His will set it in its place. How? He destined some creatures to
stay on the earth, but others to inhabit the celestial regions. He
also set in place the blessed angels, both for human salvation and
for the honor of His Name. How? By assigning some to help
humans in their need, and others to manifest to people the judgments of His secrets.

Therefore *you see in the secret places in the heights of Heaven two armies of*
heavenly spirits who shine with great brightness; thus, as is shown to you in
the height of secret places that the bodily eye cannot penetrate but
the inner sight can see, these two armies indicate that the human
body and soul should serve God, since they are going to have the
brightness of eternal blessedness with the citizens of Heaven.

On the appearance of the angels and its meaning

And those in one of the armies have on their breasts wings, with forms like human
forms in front of them, on which human features show as if in clear water. These
are the angels, who spread the desires in the depths of their
minds like wings; not that they have wings like birds, but that in
their desires they are quick to accomplish God's will, the way a

person's thoughts speed swiftly. And by their forms they display in themselves the beauty of reason, by which God closely examines human deeds; for as a servant who hears his master's words carries them out according to his will, so the angels pay attention to God's will for humans and show Him human actions in themselves.

On the appearance of the archangels and its meaning

And so those in the second army also have wings on their breasts, which display forms like human forms, in which the image of the Son of Man shines as if in a mirror. These are the archangels, who contemplate God's will in the desires of their intellect and display in themselves the beauty of reason; they magnify the Incarnate Word of God in the purest way, because, knowing God's secret decrees, they have often prefigured the mysteries of the Incarnation of the Son of God. *And you can see no other form either in these or in the others,* for in both the angels and the archangels there are many secret mysteries that the human intellect, weighed down by the mortal body, cannot understand. *But these armies are arrayed in the shape of a crown around five other armies.* This shows that the human body and soul must, by virtue of their strength, contain the five human senses, purify them by the five wounds of My Son, and lead them to the righteousness of governance from within.

On the appearance of the virtues and its meaning

And so those in the first of these five armies seem as if they have human forms that shine with great splendor from the shoulders down. These are the Virtues, which spring up in the hearts of believers and in ardent charity build in them a lofty tower, which is their works, so that in their reason they show the deeds of the elect, and in their strength bring them to a good end with a great glory of blessedness. How? The elect, whose inner understanding is clear, cast away all their wickedness of evil, being enlightened by these Virtues in the enlightenment of My will, and fight vigorously against the snares of the Devil; and these Virtues unceasingly show to Me, their Creator, these struggles against the Devil's throng. For people have within themselves struggles of confession and of denial. How? Because this one confesses Me and that one denies Me. And in this struggle the question is: Is there a God or not? And the answer comes from the Holy Spirit who dwells in the person: God is, and created you, and also redeemed you.

But as long as this question and answer are in a person, the power of God will not be absent from him, for this question and answer carries with it penitence. But when this question is not in a person, neither is the answer of the Holy Spirit, for such a person drives out God's gift from himself and, without the question that leads to penitence, throws himself upon death. And the Virtues display to God the battles of these wars, for they are the seal that shows God the intention that worships or denies Him.

On the appearance of the Powers and its meaning

Those in the second army shine with such great brightness that you cannot look at them. These are the Powers, and this means that no weak, mortal sinner can understand the serenity and beauty of the power of God or attain a likeness to it, for God's power is unfailing.

On the appearance of the Principalities and its meaning

Those in the third have the appearance of white marble and heads like human heads, over which torches are burning, and from the shoulders down they are surrounded by an iron gray cloud. These are the Principalities, and they show that those who by God's gift are rulers of people in this world must assume the true strength of justice, lest they fall into the weakness of instability. They should contemplate their Head, who is Christ the Son of God, direct their government according to His will for human needs, and seek the grace of the Holy Spirit in the ardor of truth, that until their end they may continue firm and unshaken in the strength of equity.

On the appearance of the Dominations and its meaning

Those in the fourth have forms like human forms and feet like human feet, and wear helmets on their heads, and marble tunics. These are the Dominations; they show that He who is the Lord of all has raised human reason, which had lain polluted in the dust of humanity, from earth to Heaven, when He sent to earth His Son and His Son in His righteousness trod underfoot the ancient seducer; and thus the faithful should faithfully imitate Him, who is their Head, placing their hope in Heaven and fortifying themselves with the strong desire of good works.

On the appearance of the Thrones and its meaning

And those in the fifth have nothing human in their appearance and shine red like the dawn. These are the Thrones, showing that when for human salvation the Only-Begotten of God, He who was uninfected by human sin, put on a human body, Divinity bent down to humanity; for He, being conceived by the Holy Spirit in the dawn, which is to say in the Blessed Virgin, received flesh with no spot of uncleanness whatsoever. *And you see no other form in them,* for there are many mysteries of the celestial secrets that human frailty cannot understand. *But these armies are also arrayed like a crown around two others.* This means that the faithful who direct their body's five senses to celestial things, knowing that they have been redeemed through the five wounds of the Son of God, attain with every turn and working of their mind, because they ignore the heart's pleasure and put their hope in inward things, to love of God and their neighbor.

On the appearance of the Cherubim and its meaning

Therefore those in the first of these other armies seem to be full of eyes and wings, and in each eye appears a mirror and in each mirror a human form, and they raise their wings to a celestial height. These are the Cherubim, who signify knowledge of God, by which they see the mysteries of the celestial secrets and fulfill their desires according to God's will. Thus, possessing in the depth of their knowledge the purest clarity, they miraculously foresee all those who know the true God and direct their hearts' desires, like wings on which nobly and justly to arise, to Him who is above all, and, instead of lusting after the transitory, love the eternal, as they show by the high-mindedness of their desires.

On the appearance of the Seraphim and its meaning

And those in the second army burn like fire, and have many wings, in which they show as if in a mirror all the Church ranks arrayed in order. These are the Seraphim, and this means that just as they burn for love of God and have the greatest desire to contemplate Him, they also by their desires display with shining purity the ranks, both secular and spiritual, that flourish in the mysteries of the Church, for the secrets of God show wondrously in them. Therefore all who, loving sincerity with a pure heart, seek eternal life should ardently love God and embrace Him with all their will, that they may attain to the joys of those they faithfully imitate.

But you see no other shape either in these or in the others. This is to say that there are many secrets of the blessed spirits that are not to be shown to humans, for as long as they are mortal they cannot discern perfectly the things that are eternal.

All these armies sing of the miracles God does in blessed souls

But all these armies, as you hear, are singing with marvelous voices all kinds of music about the wonders that God works in blessed souls, by which God is magnificently glorified. For spirits blessed in the power of God make known in the heavenly places by indescribable sounds their great joy in the works of wonder that God perfects in His saints, by which the latter gloriously magnify God, seeking Him in the depth of sanctity and rejoicing in the joy of salvation, as My servant David, the observer of celestial secrets, testifies when he says:

The Psalmist on this subject

"The voice of rejoicing and of salvation in the tabernacles of the just" [Ps. 118:15]. Which is to say: The song of the gladness and joy of those who tread the flesh underfoot and lift up the spirit is known, with unfailing salvation, in the dwellings of those who reject injustice and do the works of justice; they might do evil at the Devil's temptation, but by divine inspiration they do good. What does this mean? Man often has inappropriate exultation at committing an improperly desired sin; but in that state he does not have salvation, for he has gone against the divine command. He, however, who strongly does the good he ardently desires shall dance in the true exultation of the joy of salvation, for while in the body he yet loves the mansion of those who run in the way of truth and turn aside from lying error.

Therefore whoever has knowledge in the Holy Spirit and wings of faith, let this one not ignore My admonition, but taste it, embrace it, and receive it in his soul.

BOOK TWO:

The Redeemer
and Redemption

The Redeemer

And I, a person not glowing with the strength of strong lions or taught by their inspiration, but a tender and fragile rib imbued with a mystical breath, saw a blazing fire, incomprehensible, inextinguishable, wholly living and wholly Life, with a flame in it the color of the sky, which burned ardently with a gentle breath, and which was as inseparably within the blazing fire as the viscera are within a human being. And I saw that the flame sparked and blazed up. And behold! The atmosphere suddenly rose up in a dark sphere of great magnitude, and that flame hovered over it and gave it one blow after another, which struck sparks from it, until that atmosphere was perfected and so Heaven and earth stood fully formed and resplendent. Then the same flame that was in that fire and that burning extended itself to a little clod of mud that lay at the bottom of the atmosphere, and warmed it so that it was made flesh and blood, and blew upon it until it rose up a living human.

When this was done, the blazing fire, by means of the flame that burned ardently with a gentle breath, offered to the human a white flower, which hung in that flame as dew hangs on the grass. Its scent came to the human's nostrils, but he did not taste it with his mouth or touch it with his hands, and thus he turned away and fell into the thickest darkness, out of which he could not pull himself. And that darkness grew and expanded more and more in the atmosphere. But then three great stars, crowding together in their brilliance, appeared in the darkness, and then many others, both small and large, shining with great splendor, and then a gigantic star, radiant with wonderful brightness, which shot its rays toward the flame. And in the earth too appeared a radiance like the dawn, into which the flame was miraculously absorbed without being separated from the blazing fire. And thus in the radiance of that dawn the Supreme Will was enkindled.

And as I was trying to ponder this enkindling of the Will more carefully, I was stopped by a secret seal on this vision, and I heard the voice from on high saying to me, "You may not see anything further regarding this mystery unless it is granted you by a miracle of faith."

And I saw a serene Man coming forth from this radiant dawn, who poured out His brightness into the darkness; and it drove Him back with great force, so that He poured out the redness of blood and the whiteness of pallor into it, and struck the darkness such a strong blow that the person who was lying in it was touched by Him, took on a shining appearance, and walked out of it upright. And so the serene Man who had come out of that dawn shone more brightly than human tongue can tell, and made His way into the greatest height of inestimable glory, where He radiated in the plenitude of wonderful fruitfulness and fragrance.

And I heard the voice saying to me from the aforementioned living fire: "O you who are wretched earth and, as a woman, untaught in all learning of earthly teachers and unable to read literature with philosophical understanding, you are nonetheless touched by My light, which kindles in you an inner fire like a burning sun; cry out and relate and write these My mysteries that you see and hear in mystical visions. So do not be timid, but say those things you understand in the Spirit as I speak them through you, so that those who should have shown My people righteousness, but who in their perversity refuse to speak openly of the justice they know, unwilling to abstain from the evil desires that cling to them like their masters and make them fly from the face of the Lord and blush to speak the truth, may be ashamed. Therefore, O diffident mind, who are taught inwardly by mystical inspiration, though because of Eve's transgression you are trodden on by the masculine sex, speak of that fiery work this sure vision has shown you."

The Living God, then, who created all things through His Word, by the Word's Incarnation brought back the miserable human who had sunk himself in darkness to certain salvation. What does this mean?

On God's omnipotence

This blazing fire that you see symbolizes the Omnipotent and Living God, who in His most glorious serenity was never darkened by any iniquity; incomprehensible, because He cannot be divided by any division or known as He is by any part of any of His creatures' knowledge; inextinguishable, because He is that Fullness that no limit ever touched; wholly living, for there is nothing that is hidden from Him or that He does not know; and wholly Life, for everything that lives takes its life from Him, as Job shows, inspired by Me, when he says:

Words of Job on this subject

"Who is ignorant that the hand of the Lord has made all these things? In His hand is the soul of every living thing and the spirit of all human flesh" [Job 12:9–10]. What does this mean? No creature is so dull of nature as not to know what changes in the things that make it fruitful cause it to attain its full growth. The sky holds light, light air, and air the birds; the earth nourishes plants, plants fruit, and fruit animals; which all testify that they were put there by a strong hand, the supreme power of the Ruler of All, who in His strength has provided so for them all that nothing is lacking to them for their use. And in the omnipotence of the same Maker is the motion of all living things that seek the earth for earthly things, like the animals, and are not inspired by God with reason, as well as the awakening of those who dwell in human flesh and have reason, discernment, and wisdom. How?

The soul goes about in earthly affairs, laboring through many changes as fleshly behavior demands. But the spirit raises itself in two ways: sighing, groaning, and desiring God; and choosing among options in various matters as if by some rule, for the soul has discernment in reason. Hence Man contains in himself the likeness of Heaven and earth. In what way? He has a circle, which contains his clarity, breath, and reason as the sky has its lights, air, and birds; and he has a receptacle containing humidity, germination, and birth as the earth contains fertility, fruition, and animals. What is this? O human, you are wholly in every creature, and you forget your Creator; you are subject to Him as was ordained, and you go against His commands?

That the Word was and is indivisibly and eternally in the Father

You see that that fire has a flame in it the color of the sky, which burns ardently with a gentle breath, and which is as inseparably within the blazing fire as *the viscera are within a human being.* Which is to say that before any creatures were made, the Infinite Word was indivisibly in the Father; in the course of time He was to become incarnate in the ardor of charity, miraculously and without the stain or weight of sin, by the Holy Spirit's sweet freshness in the dawn of blessed virginity. But after He assumed flesh, the Word also remained inseparably in the Father; for as a person does not exist without the vital movements within his viscera, so the only Word of the Father could in no way be separated from Him.

Why the Son of God is called the Word

And why is He called the Word? Because, just as a word of command uttered by an instructor among local and transitory human dust is understood by people who know and foresee the reason he gave it, so also the power of the Father is known among the creatures of the world, who perceive and understand in Him the source of their creation, through the Word, who is independent of place and imperishable in His inextinguishable eternal life; and as the power and honor of a human being are known by his official words, so the holiness and goodness of the Father shines through the Supreme Word.

By the power of the Word of God every creature was raised up

And you see that *the flame sparks and blazes up.* This is to say that when every creature was raised through Him, the Word of God showed His power like a flash of flame; and when He became incarnate in the dawn and purity of virginity, it was as if He blazed up, so that from Him trickled every virtue of the knowledge of God, and Man lived again in the salvation of his soul.

God's incomprehensible power made the world and the different species

And the atmosphere suddenly rises up in a dark sphere of great magnitude. This is the material of creation while still formless and imperfect, not yet full of creatures; it is a sphere, for it is under the incomprehensible power of God, which is never absent from it, and by the Supernal Will it rises up in God's great power in the twinkling of an eye. *And that flame hovers over it like a workman and gives it one blow after another, which strike sparks from it, until that atmosphere is perfected and so Heaven and earth stand fully formed and resplendent.* For the Supernal Word, who excels every creature, showed that they all are subject to Him and draw their strength from His power, when He brought forth from the universe the different kinds of creatures, shining in their miraculous awakening, as a smith makes forms out of bronze, until all creatures were radiant with the loveliness of perfection, beautiful in the fullness of their arrangement in higher and lower ranks, the higher made radiant by the lower and the lower by the higher.

After the other creatures Man was created from earthly mud

But then the same flame that is in that fire and that burning extends itself to a little clod of mud that lies at the bottom of the atmosphere; this is to say that after the other creatures were created, the Word of God, in the strong will of the Father and supernal love, considered the poor fragile matter from which the weak frailty of the human race, both bad and good, was to be produced, now lying in heavy unconsciousness and not yet roused by the breath of life; *and warms it so that it is made flesh and blood,* that is, poured fresh warmth into it, for the earth is the fleshly material of humans, and nourished it with moisture, as a mother gives milk to her children; *and blows upon it until it rises up a living human,* for He aroused it by supernal power and miraculously raised up a human being with intelligence of body and mind.

Adam accepted obedience, but by the Devil's counsel did not obey

When this is done, the blazing fire, by means of the flame that burns ardently with a gentle breath, offers to the human a white flower, which hangs in that flame as dew hangs on the grass. For, after Adam was created, the Father in His lucid serenity gave to Adam through His Word in the Holy Spirit the sweet precept of obedience, which in fresh fruitfulness hung upon the Word; for the sweet odor of sanctity trickled from the Father in the Holy Spirit through the Word and brought forth fruit in greatest abundance, as the dew falling on the grass makes it grow. *Its scent comes to the human's nostrils, but he does not taste it with his mouth or touch it with his hands;* for he tried to know the wisdom of the Law with his intelligence, as if with his nose, but did not perfectly digest it by putting it in his mouth or fulfill it in full blessedness by the work of his hands. *And thus he turns away and falls into the thickest darkness, out of which he cannot pull himself.* For, by the Devil's counsel, he turned his back on the divine command and sank into the gaping mouth of death, so that he did not seek God either by faith or by works; and therefore, weighed down by sin, he could not rise to true knowledge of God until He came who obeyed His Father sinlessly and fully.

And that darkness grows and expands more and more in the atmosphere; for the power of death in the world was constantly increased by the spread of wickedness, and human knowledge entangled itself in many vices in the horror of bursting and stinking sin.

Abraham, Isaac, Jacob, and the other prophets drove back the darkness

But then three great stars, crowding together in their brilliance, appear in the darkness, and then many others, both small and large, shining with great splendor. These are the three great luminaries Abraham, Isaac, and Jacob, symbolizing the Heavenly Trinity, embracing one another both by their works of faith and by their relationship in the flesh, and by their signs driving back the darkness in the world; and, following them, the many other prophets both minor and major, radiant with many wonders.

The prophet John, glittering with miracles, foretold the Son of God

And then a gigantic star appears, radiant with wonderful brightness, which shoots its rays toward the flame. This is the greatest prophet John the Baptist, who glittered with miracles in his faithful and serene deeds and pointed out by their means the true Word, the true Son of God; for he did not yield to wickedness, but vigorously and forcefully cast it out by works of justice.

At the Incarnation of the Word of God the great counsel was seen

And in the earth too appears a radiance like the dawn, into which the flame is miraculously absorbed without being separated from the blazing fire. This is to say that God set a great splendor of light in the place where He would bring forth His Word and, fully willing it, sent Him there, yet not so as to be divided from Him; but He gave that profitable fruit and brought Him forth as a great fountain, so that every faithful throat could drink and never more be dry. *And thus in the radiance of that dawn the Supreme Will is enkindled;* for in the bright and roseate serenity was seen the fruitfulness of the great and venerable counsel, so that all the forerunners marveled at it with bright joy.

Humans must not scrutinize God's secrets beyond what He wishes to show

But you, O human, who seek in the way of humans to know more fully the loftiness of this counsel, are opposed by a concealing barrier; for you must not search into the secrets of God beyond those things the Divine Majesty wills to be revealed for love of those who trust in Him.

Christ by His death brought back His elect to their inheritance

And you see a serene Man coming forth from this radiant dawn, who pours out His brightness into the darkness; and it drives Him back with great force, so that He pours out the redness of blood and the whiteness of pallor into it, and strikes the darkness such a strong blow that the person who is lying in it is touched by Him, takes on a shining appearance, and walks out of it upright. This is the Word of God imperishably incarnate in the purity of unstained virginity and born without pain, and yet not separated from the Father. How? While the Son of God was being born in the world from a mother, He was still in Heaven in the Father; and at this the angels suddenly trembled and sang the sweetest praises of rejoicing. And, living in the world without stain of sin, He sent out into the darkness of unbelief His clear and blessed teachings and salvation; but, rejected by the unbelieving people and led to His Passion, He poured out His beautiful blood and knew in His body the darkness of death. And thus conquering the Devil, he delivered from Hell his elect, who were held prostrate there, and by His redeeming touch brought them back to the inheritance they had lost in Adam. As they were returning to their inheritance timbrels and harps and all kinds of music burst forth, because Man, who had lain in perdition but now stood upright in blessedness, had been freed by heavenly power and escaped from death, as through My servant Hosea I have stated thus:

Words of Hosea on this subject

"The iniquity of Ephraim is bound up; his sin is hidden. The sorrows of a woman in labor shall come upon him; he is an unwise son; for now he shall not stand in the contrition of the sons. I will deliver them out of the hand of death, from death I will redeem them. I will be your death, O Death; I will be your destruction, O Hell!" [Hos. 13:12–14]. What does this mean? The Devil's perverse iniquity is bound by heavy fetters, since he does not deserve that God's zeal should release him; for he has never rightfully acknowledged Him as do those who faithfully fear Him. For the Devil always raises himself against God, saying, "I am God!" and he always goes astray over the Blessed One of the Lord, opposing the name of Christians because of Him. Thus his malice is so ingrained that his sin, cruelly committed in filthy pride, can never deserve by any reparation to be covered by salvation. Therefore he will be in perpetual pain, as a woman in labor is afflicted by despair when she doubts she can survive the opening of her womb. For this misery will remain with him, that he is forsaken by beatitude because the wisdom of the sons flees from him, and he does not come to himself, as that man came to himself who returned to his father from his wickedness.

Thus he will never stand trusting in that action by which the children of salvation in the Heavenly Son crush death in its hardened iniquity, which the cunning serpent brought forth when he suggested deceit to the guileless first man. But since those children despise the poison of that unclean advice and look to their salvation, I will deliver them from slavery to idols; for idols are by their deceptiveness in the power of perdition, and for them the unfaithful forsake the honor of their Creator, entangling themselves in the Devil's snare and doing his works at his will.

And so I will redeem the souls of those who love and worship Me, the Holy and the Just, from the pain of Hell; for no one can be released from the Devil's fetters, which bind him with bitterest death by his transgression of God's precepts, except by the redemption of Him who will redeem His elect with His own blood. This is how I will slay you, O Death, with utter destruction, for I will take from you the thing you think to live by, and you will be called a useless corpse; at the height of your strength you will lie prostrate, as a corpse without the soul lies prostrate awaiting decay. For when the happy souls are mercifully raised up to celestial bliss through the new Man, who will not be a party to poisonous deception, the fountain of living water will drown you. Thus, also to your confusion, I will be your destruction, O Hell, when My strong power will take from you your ill-gotten spoils, so that you too, justly despoiled, will never again appear whole and laden with riches, but will lie prostrate and confounded forever, bearing wounds and decay.

The Son of God rising from the dead showed Man the way from death to life

And, as you see, *the serene Man who has come out of that dawn shines more brightly than human tongue can tell,* which shows that the noble body of the Son of God, born of the sweet Virgin and three days in the tomb (to confirm that there are three Persons in one Divinity), was touched by the glory of the Father, received the Spirit, and rose again to serene immortality, which no one can explain by thought or word. And the Father showed Him with His open wounds to the celestial choirs, saying, "This is My beloved Son, whom I sent to die for the people." And so joy unmeasurable by the human mind arose in them, for criminal forgetfulness of God was brought low, and human reason, which had lain prostrate under the Devil's persuasion, was uplifted to the knowledge of God; for the way to truth was shown to Man by the Supreme Beatitude, and in it he was led from death to life.

The risen Christ appeared frequently to His disciples

But just as the children of Israel, after being liberated from Egypt, wandered in the desert for forty years before coming into the land flowing with milk and honey, so too the Son of God, rising from the dead, showed Himself for forty days to His disciples and the blessed women who wept and had a great desire to see Him. This He did to encourage them, lest they should waver in faith and say, "We did not see Him, so we cannot believe that He is our salvation!" He showed Himself to them frequently to strengthen them that they might not fall.

When Christ ascended to the Father, His Bride was given many ornaments

And He makes His way into the greatest height of inestimable glory, where He radiates in the plenitude of wonderful fruitfulness and fragrance. This is to say that the Son of God ascended to the Father, who with the Son and the Holy Spirit is the height of lofty and excelling joy and gladness unspeakable; where that same Son gloriously appears to His faithful in the abundance of sanctity and blessedness, so that they believe with pure and simple hearts that He is true God and Man. And then indeed the new Bride of the Lamb was set up with many ornaments, for she had to be ornamented with every kind of virtue for the mighty struggle of all the faithful people, who are to fight against the crafty serpent.

But let the one who sees with watchful eyes and hears with attentive ears welcome with a kiss My mystical words, which proceed from Me, who am life.

The Trinity

> Then I saw a bright light, and in this light the figure of a man the color of a
> sapphire, which was all blazing with a gentle glowing fire. And that bright
> light bathed the whole of the glowing fire, and the glowing fire bathed the
> bright light; and the bright light and the glowing fire poured over the whole
> human figure, so that the three were one light in one power of potential.
>
> And again I heard the Living Light saying to me:

On the perception of God's mysteries

This is the perception of God's mysteries, whereby it can be dis-
tinctly perceived and understood what is that Fullness whose origin was never seen and in which that lofty strength never fails
that founded all the sources of strength. For if the Lord were
empty of His own vitality, what then would have been His deeds?
And therefore in the whole work it is perceived who the Maker is.

On the Three Persons

Therefore you see *a bright light*, which without any flaw of illu-
sion, deficiency, or deception designates the Father; *and in this light
the figure of a man the color of a sapphire*, which without any flaw of
obstinacy, envy, or iniquity designates the Son, who was begotten of the Father in Divinity before time began, and then within
time was incarnate in the world in Humanity; *which is all blazing
with a gentle glowing fire*, which fire without any flaw of aridity,

mortality, or darkness designates the Holy Spirit, by whom the Only-Begotten of God was conceived in the flesh and born of the Virgin within time and poured the true light into the world.

And that bright light bathes the whole of the glowing fire, and the glowing fire bathes the bright light; and the bright light and the glowing fire pour over the whole human figure, so that the three are one light in one power of potential. And this means that the Father, who is Justice, is not without the Son or the Holy Spirit; and the Holy Spirit, who kindles the hearts of the faithful, is not without the Father or the Son; and the Son, who is the plenitude of fruition, is not without the Father or the Holy Spirit. They are inseparable in Divine Majesty, for the Father is not without the Son, nor the Son without the Father, nor the Father and the Son without the Holy Spirit, nor the Holy Spirit without Them. Thus these Three Persons are one God in the one and perfect majesty of Divinity, and the unity of Their Divinity is unbreakable; the Divinity cannot be rent asunder, for it remains inviolable without change. But the Father is declared through the Son, the Son through creation, and the Holy Spirit through the Son incarnate. How? It is the Father who begot the Son before the ages; the Son through whom all things were made by the Father when creatures were created; and the Holy Spirit who, in the likeness of a dove, appeared at the baptism of the Son of God before the end of time.

People must not forget to invoke the one God in Three Persons

Hence let no person ever forget to invoke Me, the sole God, in these Three Persons, because for this reason I have made Them known to Man, that he may burn more ardently in My love; since it was for love of him that I sent My Son into the world, as My beloved John testifies, saying:

John on the charity of God

"By this the charity of God has appeared toward us: that God has sent His Only-Begotten Son into the world that we may live by Him. In this is charity, not that we have loved God, but that He has loved us and sent His Son to be a propitiation for our sins" [1 John 4:9–10]. What does this mean? That because God loved us, another salvation arose than that we had had in the beginning, when we were heirs of innocence and holiness; for the Supernal Father showed His charity in our dangers, though we deserved punishment, in sending by supernal power His Holy Word alone into the darkness of the world for the people's sake. There the Word perfected all good things, and by His gentleness brought back to life those who had been cast out because of their unclean sins and could not return to their lost holiness. What does this mean?

That through this fountain of life came the embrace of God's maternal love, which has nourished us unto life and is our help in perils, and is the deepest and sweetest charity and prepares us for penitence. How?

God has mercifully remembered His great work and His precious pearl, Man, whom He formed from the mud of the earth and into whom He breathed the breath of life. How? By devising the life of penitence, which will never fail in efficacy. For through his proud suasion the cunning serpent deceived Man, but God cast him into penitence, which calls for the humility the Devil did not know and could not practice; for he knew not how to rise up to the right way.

Hence this salvation of charity did not spring from us, and we were ignorant and incapable of loving God for our salvation; but He Himself, the Creator and Lord of all, so loved His people that for their salvation He sent His Son, the Prince and Savior of the faithful, who washed and dried our wounds. And He exuded the sweetest balm, from which flow all good things for salvation. Therefore, O human, you must understand that no misfortune or change can touch God. For the Father is the Father, the Son is the Son, and the Holy Spirit is the Holy Spirit, and these Three Persons are indivisible in the Unity of the Divinity. How?

On the three qualities of a stone

There are three qualities in a stone, three in a flame, and three in a word. How? In the stone is cool dampness and solidity to the touch and sparkling fire. It has cool dampness that it may not be dissolved or broken, solidity to the touch that it may make up habitations and defenses, and sparkling fire that it may be heated and consolidated into hardness. Now this cool dampness signifies the Father, who never withers and whose power never ends; this solidity of touch designates the Son, who was born of the Virgin and could be touched and known; and the sparkling fire signifies the Holy Spirit, who enkindles and enlightens the hearts of the faithful. What does this mean?

As a person who in the body often touches the cool dampness of stone falls sick and grows weak, so one who in his unsteady thoughts rashly tries to contemplate the Father loses his faith. And as people build their dwellings and defend themselves against their enemies by handling the solidity of stone, so too the Son of God, who is the true Cornerstone, is the dwelling of the faithful people and their protector from evil spirits. And as sparkling fire gives light to dark places by burning what it touches, so also the Holy Spirit drives out unbelief and consumes the blight of iniquity. And as these three qualities are in one stone, so the true Trinity is in the true Unity.

On the three qualities in a flame

Again, as the flame of a fire has three qualities, so there is one God in Three Persons. How? A flame is made up of brilliant light, red power, and fiery heat. It has brilliant light that it may shine, red power that it may endure, and fiery heat that it may burn. Therefore by the brilliant light understand the Father, who with paternal love opens His brightness to His faithful; by the red power, which is in the flame that it may be strong, understand the Son, who took on a body born from a Virgin, in which His divine wonders were shown; and by the fiery heat understand the Holy Spirit, who burns ardently in the minds of the faithful. But there is no flame seen where there is neither brilliant light nor red power nor fiery heat; and thus also where neither the Father nor the Son nor the Holy Spirit is known God is not properly worshiped. Therefore as these three qualities are found in one flame, so Three Persons must be understood in the Unity of the Divinity.

On the three causes of human words

And as three causes for the production of words are seen, so the Trinity in the Unity of the Divinity is to be inferred. How? In a word there is sound, force, and breath. It has sound that it may be heard, meaning that it may be understood, and breath that it may be pronounced. In the sound, then, observe the Father, who manifests all things with ineffable power; in the meaning, the Son, who was miraculously begotten of the Father; and in the breath, the Holy Spirit, who sweetly burns in Them. But where no sound is heard, no meaning is used, and no breath is lifted, there no word will be understood; so also the Father, Son, and Holy Spirit are not divided from one another, but do Their works together.

So as there are these three causes for one word, the celestial Trinity is likewise in the celestial Unity. So as in a stone there exists and there operates no cool dampness without solidity to the touch and sparkling fire, or solidity to the touch without cool dampness and sparkling fire, or sparkling fire without cool dampness and solidity to the touch; and as in a flame there exists and there operates no brilliant light without red power and fiery heat, or red power without brilliant light and fiery heat, or fiery heat without brilliant light and red power; and as in a word there exists and there operates no sound without meaning and breath, or meaning without sound and breath, or breath without sound and meaning, but all keep indivisibly together to operate; so also these Three Persons of the true Trinity live inseparably in the majesty of the Divinity and are not divided from each other.

Thus, O human, understand the One God in Three Persons. In the foolishness of your mind you think that God is so powerless that He cannot truly live in Three Persons, but only exist weakly in one. What does this mean? God is, in Three Persons, the true God, the First and the Last.

On the unity of essence

But the Father is not without the Son, or the Son without the Father, or the Father and the Son without the Holy Spirit, or the Holy Spirit without Them; for these Three Persons are inseparable in the Unity of the Divinity. How? A word sounds from a person's mouth, but the mouth does not sound without a word, nor does the word sound without life. Where does the word stay? In the person. And from whence does it go forth? From the person. And how? Because the person is living. Thus in the Father is the Son, whom the Father sent into the dark world for human salvation, conceived in the Virgin by the Holy Spirit. As the Son is the Only-Begotten in the Divinity, He is the only-begotten in virginity; as he is the Only One of the Father, He is the only-born of the Mother; as the Father begot Him before time began, the Virgin Mother bore the same Only One within time and after childbirth remained a virgin.

Therefore, O human, in these Three Persons recognize your God, who created you in the power of His Divinity and redeemed you from damnation. And do not forget your Creator, as Solomon urges you when he writes:

Words of Solomon

"Remember your Creator in the days of your youth, before the time of affliction comes, and the years draw nigh of which you shall say: They please me not" [Eccles. 12:1]. What does this mean? With your mental powers remember Him who created you when, in the days of your false confidence, you think it is possible for you to walk according to your own desires, raise yourself on high to throw yourself into the abyss, and stand in prosperity to fall into calamity. For the force of life in you always strives to perfect itself, until the time when it is complete. How? From birth a child grows up to full stature and remains an adult, leaving the mental license that is in foolish behavior and thinking carefully about how to manage his affairs, as he did not do in the foolishness of childhood. So let the person of faith do too. Let him leave childish behavior and grow up to fullness of virtue and persevere in its strength, leaving the pride of his desire, which pants after foolish vice; but let him with anxious care meditate what may be useful for him, though before he stooped childishly to childish ways.

Therefore, O human, embrace your God in the daylight of your strength, before the hour comes for the purgation of your works, when all things will be manifest and nothing will be overlooked, when the times come that will be complete and will never end, about which times your humanity murmurs a little, saying, "These changes do not please me, for I do not understand whether they will give me good fortune or calamity." For the human mind always wavers on this subject, since when it does good works it is anxious about whether or not they will please God, and when it does bad ones it is afraid to lose forgiveness and salvation.

But let the one who sees with watchful eyes and hears with attentive ears welcome with a kiss My mystical words, which proceed from Me, who am life.

BOOK THREE:

The History of Salvation Symbolized by a Building

The Edifice of Salvation

Then I saw, within the circumference of the circle, which extended from the One seated on the throne, a great mountain, joined at its root to that immense block of stone above which were the cloud and the throne with its Occupant; so that the stone was continued on to a great height and the mountain was extended down to a wide base.

And on that mountain stood a four-sided building, formed in the likeness of a four-walled city; it was placed at an angle, so that one of its corners faced the east, one faced the west, one the north, and one the south. The building had one wall around it, but made of two materials: One was a shining light like the light of the sky, and the other was stones joined together. These two materials met at the east and north corners, so that the shining part of the wall went uninterruptedly from the east corner to the north corner, and the stone part went from the north corner around the west and south corners and ended in the east corner. But that part of the wall was interrupted in two places, on the west side and on the south side.

This building was a hundred cubits long and fifty cubits wide, and the wall was five cubits high so that the two side walls were of equal length and the front and back walls were of equal length. But the four walls were equal in height except for the bulwarks, which were somewhat taller.

And between the building and the light of the circle, which extended from the height to the abyss, at the top of the east corner there was only a palm's breadth; but at the north and west and south corners, the breadth of separation between the building and the light was so great that I could not grasp its extent.

And as I was marveling, the One seated on the throne again said to me:

Faith rose in the circumcision of Abraham and climaxed in the Incarnation

Faith appeared faintly in the saints of the Old Testament, who did the justice that was constructed on high in the goodness of the Father. But at the Incarnation of the Son of God, it burst into burning light by the open manifestation of ardent deeds; for the Son of God did not desire transitory things and taught by example that they should be trampled underfoot and only celestial things loved. The early patriarchs did not flee or separate themselves from the world, for it had not yet been shown them that they should forsake all things; but they worshiped God with simple faith and humble devotion.

Therefore *you see within the circumference of the circle, which extends from the One seated on the throne, a great mountain, joined at its root to that immense block of stone above which are the cloud and the throne with its Occupant; so that the stone is continued on to a great height and the mountain is extended down to a wide base.* This is to say that the mountain, which signifies faith, stands within the mighty and strongly built power of the Supreme Father; this faith, great in virtue, first appeared in the circumcision of Abraham and progressed until the coming of the Supreme God's Son. Since the ancient serpent was ruined, this faith has been inspired in people by the Holy Spirit; faithfully working in the Father, they can believe that God is almighty, who could conquer so great an enemy, and uplifted by this belief, they can attain to that glory from which the Devil was cast out for his pride.

Faith and fear of the Lord are joined to one another

And this mountain is rooted in that immense stone, which holds the mystery of the fear of the Lord; for faith is connected to constant fear of the Lord, and fear of the Lord to the strength of faith. This is because the Son was sent from the Father to be born of the Virgin, and from the Son came forth true faith, which was the first foundation of the good works that fear of the Lord brings forth with all the virtues, whose height touches God. And so, in the wise minds of the faithful, God, who reigns over all things, is faithfully worshiped. How? Because fear of the Lord, with its sharp contemplative sight, penetrates the secrets of Heaven; for fear is the beginning of a just intention, and when that flowers into sanctity by good works, it joins with blessed faith and reaches God in full perfection.

The faithful build good works on faith in all four corners of the earth

And on that mountain stands a four-sided building, formed in the likeness of a four-walled city; which is to say that the goodness of the Father builds good works on faith. Gathering multitudes of the faithful from the four corners of the earth, he draws them to celestial things and fortifies them in constancy of virtue; then the Heavenly Father graciously places them in His bosom, which is to say in His inner power and His mystical counsel, in four categories of faith. How?

On the four categories

I who am the Most High ordained in My work the first category of people, the race of Adam, which race, after his death, went on weakened by great discord until the second arose. This was at the coming of Noah, when the Flood took place, in which, by the ark, I foretold the mysteries of My Son. But in the time of Noah, by My commands I showed the shining part of the wall of the building; by drowning sinners in the Flood, I implied to people that they should flee death and seek life and thus opened to them the knowledge of the choice between the two ways. What does this mean?

A person flourishes and thrives in the living life, which is the soul, and in it he contemplates and sees two ways, good and evil; either way is open to him, so that while he is in the body he can do good or evil with soul and body, starting with his mental choice and perfecting his will in his deeds. And so, in Noah, by My command there was shown the knowledge of the choice between the two ways and a sharp warning to spurn evil and love good. And, with the decree of circumcision, this anticipation of God's will leads to the third category, in which Abraham and Moses were united in circumcision and the Law. Circumcision and the Law continued until the fourth category, the time of the Holy Trinity, when the Old Testament was openly fulfilled in the Son of God. And so, through the Son of God an inner shoot arose in the Church; He was born and suffered for human salvation, rose again and returned to the Father, and so restored that corner of the wall that had been obscured and weakened by Adam's fall, building it up again with saved human souls.

People must go forward humbly and wisely flee the Devil's snares

But the fact that *the building is placed at an angle* means that Man, who is the work of God, is too weak to go forward by conquering the Devil by force, without fear of sin or bodily harm; he must humbly avoid the Devil, wisely flee his snares, and faithfully unite himself to good works. Thus he will be established on the Son of God, who sits in the corner and is the Cornerstone, and thus join himself to the work of human salvation.

The four corners of the building and what they mean

But *one of its corners faces the east, one faces the west, one the north, and one the south.* This means the following. The Son of God was born of the Virgin and suffered in the flesh that justice might arise and humanity be restored to life with all justice; and that is the eastern corner. From it arose the salvation of souls when in His Son God fulfilled justice, which was prefigured from the time of Abel till the coming of the Son Himself, and in Him was ended the physical observance of the laws in the Old Testament. Then came the salvation of faithful people by their faith, which in the last times the Son of God, who was sent by the Father, brought into the world, which is the western corner. In Abraham and in Moses justice raised itself against the Devil, and they foreshadowed the promised grace through which Man was saved, though the Devil had deceived him and slain him like a robber in Adam's fall, which is the northern corner. And the wretched and fatal fall of the human race was at last through heavenly grace nobly and beautifully restored, and the ardent work of God and Man bore full fruit, which is the southern corner.

Another meaning for the corners

The southern corner also means that the first man, Adam, was created by God. But the knowledge of the choice of the two roads does not come from this corner; which means that from Adam on the human race was disorderly and did not worship God in wisdom by eager service to the Law, but did its own will in great evil. It did not glow with knowledge of God or true beatitude, but lay in death; but what the Father willed to do with the human race lay hidden only in His heart. The eastern corner designates Noah, in whom justice began to show itself; thus there was openly manifested and foreshadowed the knowledge of sanctity that would later be perfected in the Son of God. And because in the Son of God, who is the true Orient, every kind of justice began, and for the sake of His sanctity and honor, first truly declared in Noah, the building should always be named starting from the east.

The northern corner also means Abraham and Moses, who, working against Satan, surrounded that knowledge as if with precious stones and roofed it in with the golden roof of God's manifest justice, which was circumcision and the Law. For, before circumcision and the Law, justice was naked and without deeds.

And the fourth, the western corner, also means the true Trinity, which showed Itself when the Savior was baptized; and He returned to Heaven with all his work to save souls and built there the true holy city Jerusalem.

God gives people fortifications and defenses of their good works

The building has one wall around it, but made of two materials: One is a shining light like the light of the sky, and the other is stones joined together. These two materials meet at the east and north corners. This is to say that the goodness of the Father gives people unbroken security in the form of a fortification and defense of their good works; and thus, surrounded and strengthened by them, people may forsake the lusts of the flesh and fly to the One God, who is their protection.

The wall is of two materials. The first is the knowledge of the choice of the two roads, which is given to people when they speculate and think clearly with their minds, to make them circumspect in all their affairs; and the second is earthy human flesh, for people were created by God to do active deeds.

On the reflective knowledge

And the knowledge *shines as brightly as daylight,* because through it people know and judge their actions, and the human mind that is carefully considering itself is radiant. For this beautiful knowledge appears in people like a white cloud and passes through human minds as swiftly as the cloud moves through the air; and it shines like daylight, because when God graciously does His most splendid work in humans and they avoid evil, the good they accomplish is as bright in them as the day.

And every human deed proceeds from this knowledge. How? Each person can have two ways. How? With his sensibilities he knows good and evil; and when he moves away from evil by doing good he imitates God, who works good in Himself, who is just and knows no injustice. But when he does evil, the wily Devil entangles him in sins, for the Devil seeks iniquity and flees sanctity and will not rest until he holds the person bound by evil deeds. But if the person breaks free of evil and does good, the Supreme Goodness will receive him, for he has conquered himself for the love of God, who handed over his Son for him to the death of the cross.

This knowledge is reflective because it is like a mirror; for as a person sees his face in a mirror and discerns beauty or blemishes, so too in the finished deeds he ponders within himself he can knowingly discern good and evil. For this discernment is part of the reason with which God inspired Man when He breathed life and soul into his body. The life of animals is deficient, because it is not rational; the human soul is never deficient, but because of its rationality it will live forever. And so a person contemplating good and evil knows whether a deed is wicked or good; he was formed by the grace of God and given reason at the beginning of creation, and in the choice of baptism and the salvation of souls in the New Testament he is restored by that same grace. As My most loving Paul says about this election of grace:

Words of Paul

"There is a remnant saved according to the election of grace. And if by grace, it is not by works; otherwise grace is no longer grace" [Rom. 11:5–6]. This is to say: The remnant, who are not inside the snare of death, shall not stoop to the Devil's example, for they were openly saved when God sent His Son to become incarnate; and this is the election of grace, manifested for human salvation. How?

The grace of God created Man, but by evil works he fell. Then the election of grace was shown in the chosen vessel, for the Son of God was born from the Virgin, and it was not possible for Him to lapse. For if a person makes something useful for himself and it is taken away from him by someone else, he will get himself something even more useful that no one will take and be content with it. And this is the way the grace of God acted. It made Adam, the first man, and the Devil drew him away from innocent deeds; but then grace brought the fullness of good works and the salvation of souls through the Son of God. But if the grace of God was the cause of salvation, then it was not caused by the merit of any human deeds. How?

There was no justice in Adam's deeds; therefore humanity would never have returned to salvation by the merit of its works, except that it was restored by grace through the works of the just Son, who was obedient to His Father and cleansed by baptism, which the Son of God gave to humanity along with good works. So in this work the grace of God collaborates with humanity, and humanity with it. And therefore the grace of God goes with this work, and the work has arisen from grace.

But if salvation arose from human merit and righteous human deeds stemmed from the people themselves and not the grace of God, grace would no longer be grace. How? Because then Man would stem from himself and not from God, and no creature would give thanks to God, and the grace of God would be nothing. But as it is, the grace of God has given people the support of reason, that they may work justice in the knowledge of good and evil; and by this knowledge they can seek the good and cast away evil and so know life and death and choose which one to stay with. As Solomon says in his knowledge of wisdom:

Words of Solomon

"He has set before you water and fire; stretch forth your hand to whichever you will" [Sir. 15:16]. This is to say: When the soul awakens God gives it a great and acute power, the knowledge of evil and good, which are water and fire. For as water overflows and conceals in its depths deadly creatures and useless things, so a person overflows with evil deeds and conceals them lest he be discovered. And as fire burns and leaves no impurity unconsumed, or as a craftsman purifies jewelry by fire to remove its rust, so too does good purify a person, melting the rust of wickedness off him. Now water and fire are inimical, extinguishing or evaporating each other. And so too does a person: He kills good by evil, or evil by good, and either way he silently hides his desires within himself and turns them over in his mind.

On the working of the two motives

And while he is mulling over these desires, the person's will makes its choice of the way he wants to go, and he stretches out his hand to it and moves along it by his deeds. He does good work by God's help through grace, and he does evil by the Devil's craft and his artful temptations; and the person himself observes his deeds by the exercise of his reason. With this reason he contemplates good and evil, and the desire rises in him to choose between the two ways, good and evil, according to his will. What does this mean?

The person has the choice in that his mind's desires reflect different things to him like a mirror, and he says to himself, "If only I could do this or that!" He has not yet done them in actuality, but he has thought about them. So he stands at the fork of two roads, with knowledge of the motives of good or evil; and as he desires so at last he does, and travels upward or downward.

Righteous institutions arose in Abraham and Moses

And the other part of the wall, as you see, is like stones joined together; which symbolizes the human race, but also designates the righteous institutions that came from the minds of people like Abraham, Moses, and the others, who were the preliminary offshoots of the Law of God and all its just additions up to the end of time. How? God works in Man and through Man; thus He sent His Son to save humanity at the end of the time of the Law, working in a sinless human body. And He took the foundation of faith on Himself and carried the whole human race with Him, even the first man, who was cast out of paradise for transgressing justice. And He achieved this wondrous deed for humanity through His Law, in which He embraced all Christians; and they make up this building in the goodness of the Father, because Man will live in the celestial Jerusalem.

Reflective knowledge began in Noah, but iniquity reigned uninterrupted

So the two kinds of wall join each other on the east and on the north. For reflective knowledge and human labor join together to end the injustice in which the human race was entangled when it forgot God. From Adam arose the raging injustice of the world before the Flood; and because of that world's iniquity, the injustice was drowned with the people in the flood of waters. And then reflective knowledge first appeared, by My inspiration, in Noah's knowledge of good as in the east corner, as was foretold. But though God's admonition flourished in Noah, bold and greedy evil arose again and marched triumphantly to the north. And the iniquity of division from God was not trodden underfoot until Abraham, in whom, as in the north corner, it was choked off and the penetrating light of God's justice arose.

And truly the shining part of the wall goes uninterruptedly from the east corner to the north corner. This is to say that reflective knowledge to fortify human minds first appeared in the east corner, that is, in the days of Noah. Before Noah, iniquity sought to do all it could to mock God, and so people followed their own lusts instead of loving to worship God; and the first descendants of Adam were completely devoured by the Devil, because the knowledge was hidden from them, until in Noah that knowledge was displayed openly. This had been foreshadowed even when the Devil was confident that the whole human race was in his power. But iniquity went on as far as the north corner, that is, until the coming of Abraham and Moses; for before them, iniquity still reigned almost supreme, not yet interrupted or defeated by the established justice of God's Law, since circumcision and the Law had not yet been given. But by these fathers the Devil began to be confounded, where previously he had reigned confidently in the world; in the words of Paul, My light-giving vessel of election:

Words of Paul

"Death reigned from Adam to Moses, even over those who had not sinned in the same way as Adam, who was a type of Him who was to come" [Rom. 5:14]. Which is to say: Death reigned, with no competitors or conquerors, from the time of Adam to the time of Moses. How? Before Moses the severity and dignity of the Law had not yet been given, except the small preview of it in the circumcision Abraham accomplished at God's command; and so deathly vice went from error to error as it pleased. But then, by God's will, there arose the strong soldier Moses, and he prepared stout weapons of justice, which destroyed the worship of death by means of the Law, which contained in itself the complete salvation of souls, because it foreshadowed the Son of God. Death indeed even ruled the innocent, who were simple and moderate and did not repeat in their actions the deeds of Adam. And Adam was a type of Him who was to come. How? God created Adam just and innocent of all thought or deed of sin; and so too the Son of God was born of the Virgin Mary, with no stains of sin.

Righteousness is shown in Abraham and Moses, justice in the Incarnation

But you see that *the stone part goes from the north corner around the west and south corners and ends in the east corner.* This means that the righteous works of humans, with which God fortified them, came forth from the north corner, which is to say from the circumcision of Abraham and the Law of Moses and the justice they inspired in people. They continued to the west corner, where open justice arose in the Incarnation of the Son of God; went on from there to the south corner, where through baptism and the other just works of the newly chosen Bride of the Son of God ardent deeds were enkindled to restore Adam to salvation; and at last returned to the east corner, to end restored to the Supreme Father. How? The Supreme Father in His mystery ordained every work of justice that would bring the first, fallen man back into salvation by a return to God. How? Man had fallen, and so I arose in mercy and sent My Son to restore salvation to souls, as My servant the psalmist David shows, saying:

Words of David

"His will is in the law of the Lord, and on that law he shall meditate day and night" [Ps. 1:2]. Which is to say that the will of the Father to save is contained in the law of justice His Only-Begotten showed to the world, who is One God with the Father and the Holy Spirit and rules the whole globe. And He, the Son of the Father, was incarnate and seen as a visible Man, and in the flesh was uplifted above all creatures. How? The Son of God was begotten of His Father before all worlds and later, in the last times, born into the world of a mother; but while He was not yet incarnate He remained invisible within the Father as the will is invisible in a person before it is shown in a deed, and then later appeared visibly in the flesh for human salvation.

So the Almighty Father meditates with His Son upon an act of justice to counter the original fall of Adam. Where? In the love of His Son, who was before time began in the Father in the glory of Divinity, and then became miraculously incarnate at the appointed epoch of the world, when the Father sent Him from His heart into the world as the High Priest of all justice. Therefore the Son embodied the law of justice, as He received it from the Father when Christian law was made.

And on that law, which the Father willed to establish and make through His Son, He meditates by day. How? He Himself is the Day; and in that Day, before He made any transitory creature and while no darkness or iniquity existed in any creation of His, He meditated on His Son's law.

And also by night. How? Because when evil arose in His creatures, which is like the darkness of night in angels and people, the Father continued to meditate, and will do so until the last day, as long as His ineffable works shall last; He shows and reveals the law of His Son when in Him He perfects all the good deeds that are to be perfected in Man.

Christ's members and the Church still lack the perfection they will have

But you see that *the stone part of the wall is interrupted in two places, on the west side and on the south side.* This is to say that the work of the human race to fortify its defenses is still unfinished in two areas. The members of the Son of God, His chosen, remain imperfect, which is to say that the west side is interrupted, since from there the Son of God was sent in these last times into the world. And the Church is also still imperfect in virtue, not as she will be set up and established in the celestial Jerusalem, so that the south side is interrupted, for the Church will be perfected in Heaven.

The number ten, diminished by Adam, is multiplied again by Christ

This building is a hundred cubits long, which means that the mystical number ten was diminished by humanity when it transgressed, but was restored by My Son and multiplied by ten to a hundred as virtues were multiplied in the salvation of souls. And from the hundred, again multiplied by the ten, there will come the perfect number one thousand, referring to the virtues that will completely destroy the thousand arts of the Devil, which now seduce the whole flock of Almighty God's lovely sheep. What does this mean?

I, the Omnipotent, in the beginning made lights that burned and lived, shining in splendor, some of which stood fast in My love, but some despised Me, their Creator, and fell. But it did not befit Me, the Creator, to discard what I had made as useless and ruined. How? A part of the angelic creation grew proud of the good the Creator gave it that it might know Him and decided that it could take on false glory and be like its Creator; and so it fell into death. Then God foresaw that what had fallen in this lost group could be more firmly restored in another. How? He created Man from the mud of the earth, living in soul and body, to attain to that glory from which the apostate Devil and his followers were cast out. Man is thus exceedingly dear to God, who made him truly in His own image and likeness; he was to exercise all the virtues in the perfection of holiness, as indeed God formed all creatures to do, and to work in humble obedience to do acts of virtue, and so to fulfill the function of praise among the more glorious orders of angels. And thus in this height of blessedness he was to augment the praise of the heavenly spirits who praise God with assiduous devotion, and so fill up the place left empty by the lost angel who fell in his presumption.

And so Man symbolizes the full number ten, perfecting these things by the power of God. But in this figure ten is multiplied to a hundred. For Man was seduced by the Devil and fell away from God; but at last he was admonished by divine mercy and inspiration, began to acknowledge God in the law and prophecy of the Old Testament, and then attained more insight by the sanctity and the means of constancy in virtue given by the Church.

And so, starting with Abel, Man began to practice all the virtues, and will continue to perfect them until the day of the last just person; and this is why the length of the building is the number one hundred, which God shows to humanity in a mystical figure, that it may not despair if it falls back into iniquity, but rise above it and vigorously do the work of God. For anyone who falls into sin but then rises from it again will be stronger than he was before, as God gave greater and stronger virtues to humanity by sending His Son into the world to raise up the prostrate human race than it had had before.

And therefore people work more strongly in soul and body than if they had no difficulty in doing it, since they struggle against themselves in many perils; and, waging these fierce wars together with the Lord God, who fights faithfully for them, they conquer themselves, chastising their bodies, and so know themselves to be in His army. But an angel, lacking the hardships of an earthly body, is a soldier of Heaven only in its harmonious, lucid, and pure constancy in seeing God, while a human, handicapped by the filth of his body, is a strong, glorious, and holy soldier in the work of restoration, which he does in soul and body for the sake of God. And so by the number one hundred of his present labor he attains to the one thousand of future repayment; on the last day he will receive his full and eternal reward and rejoice in soul and body without end in the celestial habitations. And so the diminished ten is recovered through My Son, who was born of the Virgin, suffered on the cross, and brought back humanity to the realms of Heaven. As My Son says in the Gospel:

Words of the Gospel

"What woman who has ten coins, if she loses one of them, does not light a candle, and sweep the house until she finds it? And when she has found it, she calls together her friends and neighbors, and says, 'Rejoice with me, for I have found my coin that was lost'" [Luke 15:8–9]. Which is to say: The Holy Divinity had ten coins, namely, ten orders of the heavenly hierarchy, including the chosen angels and Man. It lost one coin when Man fell into death by following the Devil's temptations instead of the divine precepts. Hence the Divinity kindled a burning lamp, namely, Christ, who was true God and true Man and the splendid Sun of Justice; and with Him He swept the house, namely, the Jewish people, and searched the Law for all the meaning of salvation, established a new sanctification, and found His coin, Man, whom He had lost. Then He called together His friends, namely, earthly deeds of justice, and His neighbors, namely, spiritual virtues, and said, "Rejoice with Me in praise and joy and build the celestial Jerusalem with living stones, for I have found Man, who had perished by the deception of the Devil!"

The five wounds of Christ wipe out human sins

And you see that the building is fifty cubits wide, which is to say that the whole breadth of the vices of humanity, which should have built on and revered the work of God but instead followed its own lusts, is mercifully wiped out and forgiven by the five wounds that My Son suffered on the cross. So the wounds of His hands obliterated the deed of disobedience done by the hands of Adam and Eve; the wounds of His feet cleared the path of exile for humanity to return; and the wound of His side, from which sprang the Church, wiped out the sin of Eve and Adam after Eve was made from Adam's side. And therefore My Son was nailed to the tree, to abolish what had been done through the tree that occasioned sin; and therefore He drank vinegar and gall, to take away the taste of the harmful fruit.

The Holy Spirit made Man's five senses able to know good and evil

The wall was five cubits high, which refers to the virtue of divine knowledge of the Scriptures, which imbue Man's five senses for the sake of the work of God. The Holy Spirit breathed on them for people's good, for with the five senses people can regard the height of Divinity and discern both good and evil.

Soul and body must work to avoid evil and do good in all circumstances

Thus *the two side walls are of equal length*, for, contained within the edifice of God's goodness, people must work with great constancy with the two side walls of soul and body flanking them. How? To avoid evil and do good. How? The profound and incomprehensible power of God created Man to worship God with all his strength and all his might and with all the devotion of his intelligent reason; and it is right that the Creator of all things should, before and above everything, be worshiped worthily as God.

The mind must have the wisdom and discernment to know God

Therefore *the front and back walls are of equal length*, for in the work of God wisdom and discretion are like two walls, with wisdom as the higher part and discretion as the lower. And God imbues the whole of the human mind with these, an equitable and just gift, that the mind may know Him.

People should gain devout faith from considering the four elements

But the four walls are equal in height, except for the bulwarks, which are somewhat taller. This is to say that Man, living as he does among the four elements, should hold high the Catholic faith with constant devotion and veneration through the goodness of the Father; he should worship the Son with the Father and the Holy Spirit, as the Son does all Their works in Them. How? Every work that the Son of God has done and is doing, He perfects through the goodness of the Father in the Holy Spirit. What does this mean? According to the will of the Father, the Son in His great goodness redeemed humanity through His Incarnation; for the Father ordained that the Son should be born of the Virgin, conceived by the Holy Spirit, and assume humanity for love of Man to bring him back to restored life. Therefore Man has a part in God and can enter into salvation with Him, if he has the true Catholic faith and knows the Father, the Son, and the Holy Spirit as the one true God.

The faithful person ascends from virtue to virtue

The bulwarks are much higher. How? Because when a person regards the height of goodness in his mind, he then builds a high wall of faith by virtue of the work of God. Then he ascends above that rational faith, which shows him God in the power of His Divinity, and on it he builds bulwarks of virtue higher than the wall. How? He finds that it is not enough to have faith in God and so builds virtues that rise higher; and so he grows, like a flourishing palm tree, from virtue to virtue, and by these virtues his righteous faith is exalted and adorned as bulwarks do a city.

The Father sent his Son into the world to do His will and redeem Man

And between the building and the light of the circle, which extends from the height to the abyss, at the top of the east corner there is only a palm's breadth. This is the width of the heavenly secrets that lie between the work of the Son of God when He lived in the world and did divine works, here shown as a building, and the power of the Father, which expands in mighty splendor into the places below and the places above. He sent His Son into the world to be the capstone of the corner that faces east, made up of the justice first prefigured in Noah and perfected in the Incarnation of the Son. Thus these secrets were, so to speak, just a hand's breadth wide, the distance from the thumb to the little finger of the flat hand; and that was the time ordained in the heart of the Father when He willed to send His Son. He sent Him with a strong hand and surrounded Him with all the joints of His fingers, which are His works in the Holy Spirit, that He might accomplish the will of His Father and suffer upon the cross for the wretched and contemptible disobedience with which the Devil inspired the first man. To redeem that man from that sin God's mercy bent down to earth, and the incomprehensible height of Divinity was contained in the humanity of the Son of God.

The defeat of evil and the goals of justice are secrets of God's will

But at the north and west and south corners the breadth of separation between the building and the light is so great that you cannot grasp its extent. This is to say that no one weighed down by a mortal body can understand the elation of evil in the heart of the Devil in the north; or its consummation in active creatures in the west of fallen Man; or the beginning or end of the supernal justice, which is the ardent south. Nor can such a one see how these things are worked out and differentiated between the deeds of all peoples and the power of My knowledge. Both the elect and the reprobate are subjected to a just scrutiny and examined most diligently and strictly on their obedience to My precepts; and all should trust in Me to feed them in all their needs. But all these things are so hidden in My secret counsels that human senses and understanding can never take in or understand the extent of their profundity, except as far as is granted by My permission.

But let the one who has ears sharp to hear inner meanings ardently love My reflection, pant after My words, and inscribe them in his soul and conscience.

The Pillar of the Word of God

And then, beyond the tower of anticipation of God's will, one cubit past the corner that faces the north, attached to the outside of the shining part of the main wall of the building, I saw a pillar the color of steel, most dreadful to behold, and so big and tall that I could not form an idea of its measurements. And the pillar was divided from bottom to top into three sides, with edges sharp as a sword; the first edge faced the east, the second the north, and the third the south, and the latter was somewhat merged with the outside wall of the building.

From the edge that faced the east, branches grew out from the root to the summit. At the root I saw Abraham sitting on the first branch, then Moses on the second, then Joshua on the third, and then the rest of the patriarchs and prophets, one above the other on each branch, sitting in the order in which they succeeded each other in time. They were all looking toward the edge of the pillar that faced the north, marveling at the things they could see with spiritual vision going on there in the future.

But between the two edges, the one facing the east and the one facing the north, the side of the pillar to which those patriarchs and prophets turned their faces was from bottom to top as round as if turned in a lathe and wrinkled like the bark of a tree that puts forth shoots.

And from the second edge, facing the north, there went forth a marvelously bright radiance, which shone and reflected as far as the edge that faced the south. And in the radiance, which was so widely diffused, I saw apostles, martyrs, confessors, virgins, and many other saints, walking in great joy.

And the third edge, facing the south, was broad and wide in the middle, but thinner and narrower at the bottom and top, like a bow drawn and ready to shoot arrows. And at the top of the pillar I saw a light so bright that human tongue cannot describe it; and in this light appeared a dove, with a gold ray coming out of its mouth, which shed brilliant light on the pillar.

And as I looked at this, I heard from Heaven a terrifying voice rebuking me and saying, "What you see is divine!" And at this voice I trembled so much that I dared not look there any longer.

Then I saw inside the building a figure standing on the pavement facing this pillar, looking sometimes at it and sometimes at the people who were going to and fro in the building. And that figure was so bright and glorious that I could not look at her face or her garments for the splendor with which she shone; I saw only that, like the other virtues, she appeared in human form.

And around her I saw a beautiful multitude, with the appearance and wings of angels, standing in great veneration, for they both feared and loved her. And before her face I saw another multitude, with the appearance of human beings, in dark clothes; and they stood immobile with fear.

And the figure looked upon the people who came in from the world and in the building put on a new garment, and she said to each of them, "Consider the garment you have put on, and do not forget your Creator who made you."

And as I wondered at these things, the One seated on the throne spoke to me again:

The austerity of the Law was sweetened by the Incarnation of the Word

The Word of God, by whom all things were made, was Himself begotten before time in the heart of the Father; but afterward, near the end of time, as the Old Testament saints had predicted, He became incarnate of the Virgin. And, assuming humanity, He did not forsake Deity; but, being one and true God with the Father and the Holy Spirit, he sweetened the world with His sweetness and illumined it with the brilliance of His glory.

Hence, *the pillar you see beyond the tower of anticipation of God's will* designates the ineffable mystery of the Word of God, for in that true Word, the Son of God, all the justice of the New and Old Testaments is fulfilled. This justice was opened to believers for their salvation by divine inspiration, when the Son of the Supreme Father deigned to become incarnate of the sweet Virgin; and the virtues showed themselves to be powerful in the anticipation of God's will, which was the beginning of the circumcision. Then the mystery of the Word of God was also declared in strict justice by the voice of the patriarchs and prophets, who foretold that He would be manifest in justice and godly deeds and great severity, doing the justice of God and leaving no injustice free to evade the commands of the Law.

The patriarchs in a mystery showed that the Law was near

And you see that the pillar *is standing one cubit past the corner that faces the north,* which symbolizes in human terms how very near the patriarchs who announced the strict justice of the Word of God were in their meaning to the Law, thus resisting the Devil in the north.

No pride can resist the strength of God

The pillar *is the color of steel and attached to the outside of the shining part of the main wall of the building;* for the power of the Word of God is unconquered and unconquerable, and no one can resist Him by vain rebellion or vile pride. And so the Old Testament fathers were united with the reflective knowledge, as it were, on the outside, by their bulwarks and deeds of justice; but they were not yet imbued with the fiery perfection of the work that arose in the Son of God and that they but foreshadowed outwardly in their words.

God's justice is dreadful and exceeds every creature in height

It is most dreadful to behold, for the justice in the Word of God is fearful to humans, who know only the impious judgment of unjust judges judging according to their own whims. *It is so big and tall that you cannot form an idea of its measurements,* for the Word, who is the Son of God, exceeds all creatures in paternal majesty by the magnitude of His glory and the height of His Divinity, and no human in a corruptible body can fully understand Him.

The Word of God has three divisions: Law, Grace, and exposition of scripture

And the pillar is divided from bottom to top into three sides, with edges sharp as a sword; which is to say that the strength of the Word of God as prefigured in the Old Testament and declared in the New, circling and turning in grace, showed in the Holy Spirit three points of division. These were the old Law, the new Grace, and the exposition of the faithful doctors; and by these the holy person does what is just from the beginning, starting with the good and moving upward to end with the perfect. For all that is just was, is, and will be forever in the simple Deity, which is in all things; and no power can stand firm in malice, if He wills to conquer it by the glory of His loving-kindness.

The knowledge of Law, the work of the Gospel, and the wisdom of the doctors

The first edge faces the east, which signifies the start of the knowledge of God through the divine Law, before the perfect day of justice. *The second looks to the north,* for after this good and chosen work was started there came the Gospel of My Son and the other precepts of Me, the Father, which rose up against the north, where injustice originated. *And the third faces the south and is somewhat merged with the outside wall of the building.* This is to say that when the works of justice had been confirmed, there came the profound and rich wisdom of the principal doctors, who through the fire of the Holy Spirit made known what was obscure in the Law and the Prophets and showed their fruition in the Gospels. Thus they made these things fruitful to the understanding; they touched on the outward content of the Scriptures in the work of the Father's goodness and sweetly ruminated on their mystical significance.

God worked from the beginning of the Law to the manifestation of his Son

And from the edge that faces the east, branches grow out from the root to the sum- mit. This is to say that when God first became known through the just Law, branches appeared on that eastern edge, which was the time of the patriarchs and prophets. For this sharp-edged pillar of Divinity carries on the work from its root, which is the good beginning in the minds of the elect, to its summit, which is the manifestation of the Son of Man, who is all justice.

And therefore *at the root you see Abraham sitting on the first branch,* for the time of inspiration by God began with Abraham, when he obeyed God and with a tranquil mind departed from his country. *Then Moses on the second,* for after this, God inspired Moses to plant the Law and so foreshadow the Son of the Most High. *Then Joshua on the third,* for he afterward had the spirit of the Lord in him in order to strengthen the custom of the Law as God commanded.

And then you see *the rest of the patriarchs and prophets, one above the other on each branch, sitting in the order in which they succeeded each other in time;* for God inspired each patriarch and prophet in his own time to nurture his particular shoot toward the height of His commands, and all in their day reposed on the disposition and order of the justice He showed them, faithful and obedient to the Divine Majesty as it showed itself in their times.

The patriarchs and prophets marveled at the Incarnation

They are all looking toward the edge of the pillar that faces the north, marveling at the things they can see with spiritual vision going on there in the future. For they were all alerted in their souls by the Holy Spirit, and so turned and saw how the Gospel doctrine repulsed the Devil by the strength of the Son of God. They spoke of His Incarnation and marveled at how He came from the heart of the Father and the womb of a virgin and showed Himself with great wonders both by Himself and by His followers, who wonderfully imitated Him in new grace and trod the transitory underfoot, greatly thirsting for the joys of the eternal.

The Word of God was hidden by prevision in the souls of the elect of old

But between the two edges, the one facing the east and the one facing the north, the side of the pillar to which those patriarchs and prophets are turning their faces is from bottom to top as round as if turned in a lathe and wrinkled like the bark of a tree that puts forth shoots. This is to say that between the two edges, which are the manifest knowledge of Me and the teachings of My Son, the One Word, which is My Son, was hidden as a foreshadowing image in the souls of the ancient fathers who abided in My laws, from the first chosen one until the last holy one. Thus they were decorated all around with mystical ornaments, for He carefully arranged and polished all His chosen instruments and showed Himself to them all with swift grace. He was loving to them all, as is prefigured in the wrinkles of the circumcision, which was the shadow of things to come; for it contained, hidden in the austerity of the Law, the apposite meaning of the most righteous offshoot, the high and holy Incarnation.

The words of the Son go from and return to the Father through the doctors

And from the second edge, facing the north, there goes forth a marvelously bright radiance, which shines and reflects as far as the edge that faces the south. This is to say that from the second edge, which is the New Testament and stands opposed to the Devil, there issue the words of My Son, which come forth from Me and return to Me. For when the Sun, which is My Son, stands forth in the flesh, the light of the holy Gospel shines in His preaching, pours itself out from Him and His disciples as fruits of blessing, and then returns into the fountain of salvation, where it reaches the guides, those who profoundly search into the words of the Old and New Testaments. And they show how wisdom is raised up in that Sun, who enlightens the world and burns like noonday in His elect.

The apostles, martyrs, and other elect were made so by Christ's teaching

And in the radiance, which is so widely diffused, you see apostles, martyrs, confessors, virgins, and many other saints, walking in great joy. For in the clear light in which My Son preached and spread the truth there have grown up apostles who announce that true light, martyrs who faithfully shed their blood like strong soldiers, confessors who officiate after My Son, virgins who follow the Supernal Branch, and all My other elect who rejoice in the fountain of happiness and the font of salvation, baptized by the Holy Spirit and ardently going from virtue to virtue.

Gospel knowledge was limited, is now broad, and will grow weak at the end

And the third edge, facing the south, is broad and wide in the middle, but thinner and narrower at the bottom and top, like a bow drawn and ready to shoot arrows. This is to say that, as the Gospel was spread, the wisdom of the saints broadened; they burned in the Holy Spirit, seeking It in depth so as to find through It the deepening of their understanding of the Word of God, strengthened by the faith of the Christian people. And so the sense of the Scriptures that went forth from the mouth of the holy doctors broadened too; they searched the depths of the Scriptures' astringency and made it known to the many who learned from them, and thus they too enlarged their senses by knowing more of the wisdom and knowledge of the divine writings. At the beginning of the Church's institution—as it were, at the bottom of the edge—this knowledge was narrower and less studied, for the people did not yet embrace it with the love they gave it afterward. And at the end of time—as it were, at the edge's summit—the studies of many will grow cold; divine wisdom will not be lovable to them as deeds are lovable, but they will hide their knowledge and keep it for themselves, as if they had no obligation to do good works. For they will know it only on the outside, as in a dream.

People must begin good works timidly, continue strongly, and finish humbly

And therefore *the edge is widest and sharpest in the middle.* For the austere works of the worship of God were denuded of their Old

Testament darkness and grew from their narrow beginning to their middle, which consists of the strongest virtues and the loftiest zeal. For the people were then swifter against iniquity, wounding the Devil with words from God and casting out and trampling down all his vices with the great austerity of God's justice. But then the people forgot themselves, declined, and, as the end of the world drew near, lived in a narrower fervor for the Holy Spirit. So, as a bow is stretched tight by the bowstring in time of war, a person must rise up against vice in body and soul, more constricted at each end and broader in the middle; so that the beginning and the end of his work may be circumspect with fear and humility, while its middle is strong and constant, sending forth by the gift of the Holy Spirit the darts of good deeds against the ambushes of the Devil. For when a person begins to do good, his strength is fragile; then when he continues to work good he grows stronger, because the Holy Spirit has poured Itself out in him; but since that power cannot come often, at the end of his good work he will be less in strength again because of the weakness of the flesh. And so the bow should always be bent for defense against the vices of the Devil.

God shows people the mysteries of the Son of God by foreshadowing

But at the top of the pillar you see a light so bright that human tongue cannot describe it. This is to say that the Heavenly Father, in His highest and deepest mysteries, made known the mystery of His Son, who shines in His Father with glorious light, in which there appears all the justice of the giving of the Law and the New Testament. And the latter is of such clarity and brilliance of wisdom that it is not possible for any earthly person to express it in words, as long as he is in corruptible flesh.

And in this light appears a dove, with a gold ray coming out of its mouth, which sheds brilliant light on the pillar; for in the heart of the radiant Father, in the brilliance of the light of the Son of God, burns the Holy Spirit, who comes from on high and declares the mysteries of the Son of the Most High to redeem the people seduced by the ancient serpent. And so the Holy Spirit inspires all the commandments and all the new testimonies, giving before the Incarnation of the Lord the law of His glorious mysteries, and then showing the same glory in the Incarnation itself. And the Spirit's inspiration is a golden splendor and a high and excellent illumination, and by this outpouring It makes known, as was said, the mystical secrets of God's Only-Begotten to the ancient heralds who showed the Son of God through types and marveled at His coming from the Father and His miraculously arising in the dawn of the perpetual Virgin. And thus the Spirit in Its power fused the Old Testament and the Gospels into one spiritual seed, from which grew all justice.

And so you cannot contemplate the divine glory because of the immense power of Divinity; no mortal can see it except those to whom I will to foreshadow it. Therefore take care not to presume rashly to look at what is divine, as the trembling that seizes you shows.

The virtue of the knowledge of God

And you see inside the building a figure standing on the pavement facing this pillar. This is to say that a virtue shows itself within the work of God the Father, which declares the mystery of the Word of God, for it has revealed all the justice in the city of the Omnipotent to the people of the Old and New Testaments. She is standing on the pavement, which is to say above all earthly things in the work of the loving Father, for everything in earth and Heaven are foreseen by Him.

And she looks sometimes at the pillar and sometimes at the people who are going to and fro in the building. This is to say that she is contemplating in the Word of God the mystery put forth by His power, and also the people who are working in the Father's goodness, and which of them are succeeding or not succeeding in the work, for she knows the nature of each one at will.

And this image signifies the knowledge of God; for she oversees all people and all things in Heaven and earth. And she *is so bright and glorious that you cannot look at her face or her garments for the splendor with which she shines.* For she is terrible with the terror of the avenging lightning and gentle with the goodness of the bright sun; and both her terror and her gentleness are incomprehensible to humans, the terror of divine brilliance in her face and the brightness of her beauty in her garments, as the sun cannot be looked at in its burning face or its beautiful clothing of rays. But she is with everyone and in everyone, and so beautiful is her secret that no person can know the sweetness with which she sustains people and spares them in inscrutable mercy; she spares even the hardest stone, which is a hard and incorrigible person who never wants to turn aside from evil, until it can be penetrated no farther.

But, like the other virtues, she appears in human form. For God in the power of His goodness profoundly imbued Man with reason, knowledge, and intellect, that he might dearly love and devotedly worship Him, spurn the illusions of demons, and adore Him above all who gave him such high honor.

The angels that surround her and why they are winged

And around her you see a beautiful multitude, with the appearance and wings of angels, standing in great veneration, for they both fear and love her. Which is to say that all the blessed and excellent spirits in the heavenly ministry worship the Knowledge of God with inexpressibly pure praise, as humans cannot worthily do while they are in mortal bodies. These spirits embrace God in their ardor, for they are living light; and they are winged, not in the sense that they have wings like the flying creatures, but in the sense that they circle burningly in their spheres through the power of God as if they were winged. And so they adore Me, the true God, and persevere in proper fear and true subjection, knowing My judgments and burning in My love; for they behold My face forever and desire and will nothing but those things they see are pleasing to My penetrating vision.

On human beings who are called "compelled sheep"

And before her face you see another multitude, with the appearance of human beings, in dark clothes; and they stand immobile with fear. These are people who live in the knowledge of God. How? That person whom God foresees will belong to Him stands in great honor in His sight, but one who chooses to stay in perdition rather than in God is lost. Those people you see in this multitude are called "compelled sheep"; they have a human form because of their human deeds, and dark clothes because they have done sinful works in doubt, but they fear the judgment of God with a stringent fear. They are called "compelled sheep" because I compel them by many means to come to life and be snatched from death through My Son's blood. Thus "compelled sheep" are those people who are compelled by Me against their will, by many tribulations and sorrows, to leave their iniquities. These they gladly embraced in the desire of their flesh and the flower of their youth as long as they held to the world, wanting to retain the heat of lust until the fire of the flesh departed from them in old age; but I forced them all in different ways, according to what I saw in them, to cease from their sins.

God constrains some gently, some by a strong lash, some by extreme pain

Some of these, in whom desire for the world does not burn so fiercely, I force with a lighter rather than a heavier scourge; for I do not perceive in them the great bitterness I see in others, since when they feel My correction they renounce the pomps of the world and hastily leave their own will and come to Me. Others I correct with heavier blows, since they so burn and yearn for the sins of their vicious flesh that they would not be fit for the Kingdom unless I forcibly compelled them. And My knowledge sees and knows these, and constrains them in proportion to their bodily excesses.

And others, again, I conquer by the greatest and sharpest misery of mind and body, for they are so rebellious and so extreme in their carnal pleasures that, if they were not constrained by the heaviest calamity, the wantonness of their flesh would lead them to unceasing crime. These never turn to God while their wills prosper; some fall into desperation through timidity of mind, but others are mocked by prideful ambition; and the former allow despair to trample them underfoot, while the latter cannot contain themselves for the overabundance of their spirits. So, when those who belong to Me resist Me by their deeds, I force them as My knowledge of them directs; and so, through the physical and spiritual calamities they suffer, they are compelled to come to Me and be saved. Thus Pharaoh, having been greatly terrified, finally made the Israelites go forth from his land, as it is written:

Example of Pharaoh, Moses, and Aaron

"And Pharaoh, calling Moses and Aaron by night, said, 'Rise up, go forth from my people, both you and the children of Israel. Go, sacrifice to the Lord as you say. Take your flocks and your herds as you asked, and as you depart bless me'" [Exod. 12:31–32]. Which is to say: The heavy and burdensome crimes inseparable from this world weigh people down with sorrows and miseries; they say in their hearts, "Alas, alas! Whither shall we flee?" Then these sorrows clash and drive the people away from them, and the people hasten to withdraw; for their bodies are shriveling up from the weight of the scourge in the hand of God, and they cannot live with joy amid the pleasures of the world. For God claims them, calling the just by the many calamities of the dark deeds of the night of sin.

Hence Pharaoh, which is to say, the vices of the Devil, amid the clamor of grief and misery calls Moses, which means those people whom God constrains by the keenest spiritual or physical sorrows, and Aaron, that is, those people whom He compels by lighter adversities and calls out of the night of evil deeds; and the vices say from amid the oppression of human pleasure, "Arise from your carnal habits, and go forth from the ancient dwelling place you had with us; separate yourselves from the common people whom we possess and who worship us. Separate yourselves from the secular affairs to which we gladly cling, you who were terrified by us when you were our prisoners, and take the children of God with you, who see and acknowledge Him.

"Go therefore by another way; leave us, and offer yourselves to God by means of those invincible fights in which you say you have conquered us by your will. In the newness of mind you now seek, assume the gentleness of the sheep, which prevents you from acting with us because you choose the sorrows of following the Lamb, and assume the victorious arms of the strength of herds, which we cannot resist and which have conquered us. Separate yourselves from us, as you wished when you fiercely fought us; go to the country you long for in your minds, embrace the new life that takes you from us, and bless and praise God for that battle by which you have torn yourselves away from worldly matters and cares."

How God, scrutinizing people, chastises and consoles them

And I, Almighty God, in compelling these sheep to come over to Me, strengthen My pillars, which are the strong heirs to Heaven, on a foundation of chastisement. I chastise them according to the degree of wickedness by which they are assailed and implicated in the sin of Adam; for if I do not confirm them by My grace, they cannot stand. Some who are not weighed down by a very great burden of vice I punish more lightly, for if I were to correct them with a sharper blow, their spirits would entirely fail and they would fall into desperation. For they are not bound by the force of the great whirlwind of the Devil's temptations.

But others who in the battle with the Devil are burdened with a greater weight and have savage ways and excessive lusts I constrain harshly with heavy sufferings, so that they will not withdraw from My covenant; for they belong to it and wish with all their hearts to lay hold on Me and observe My precepts. But if I chastised these as lightly as the first, they would count My corrections as nothing, for they are assailed by the ancient's serpent's most heavy attack.

And there are also certain people whom I do not know, exiles from the heavenly country, for they completely abandon Me, seducing themselves in the greed of their thoughts with devouring rage. These do not seek Me or desire to know Me, but choke off their good desires; and so they ask no help from Me, but greedily feast on their own goods and please themselves in carnal lusts.

Now some of these latter express their will in excesses and pleasures of the flesh, but do not live in hatred and envy; they are simply engulfed in sweet joys and carnal delights. To these I give the fruits of the earth in prosperity and do not let them lack and be poor, for they were created by Me and they do not devour My people with malice. And so what they choose is given to them.

But others are fierce and bitter, full of gall and hatred and envy, rendering evil for evil and suffering no injury to be inflicted on them; and if these obtain worldly honor and riches, they destroy the heavenly virtues in others and do not let them grow. And so from these I take fruits and riches and throw them into great miseries, so that they cannot do as much evil as they would want to; for, if they could, they would do the works of the Devil.

And so by a just measure I mark out the ways of good and bad people and weigh their wills according to what My eye sees of their desires, as Wisdom testifies through Solomon, saying:

Words of the wisdom of Solomon

"All human ways are open to His eyes; the Lord is the weigher of spirits" [Prov. 16:2]. Which is to say: To the sight of Almighty God all roads are open that the living human mind can choose in the present state of its wisdom, for each person possesses the knowledge of fruitful utility and of vain foolishness. Thus God sees all things, and nothing is hidden from His divine sight; He knows and observes all things, and so He can deal rightly with each and every case. How? He is the weigher of spirits; He treats them tenderly with sweet caresses and peace, or He chastises them with the tribulations of misery and sorrow that they may be conformed to the right measure. They cannot escape Him by running or fleeing, unless He so wills it in accordance with their merits; for they are weighed, both in this world and in the world to come, by the way in which they worshiped God.

And so these spirits are weighed justly, and a person's mind is uplifted to higher things or sunk to lower things exactly as far as God's just judgment requires. No soul has enough power to fight against God, who resists their attempts, for He judges all things most righteously and opposes them with His irresistible justice, so that they can do no more than He permits.

And as the leaden counterweight weighs money correctly, so God in His equal scales counterbalances the good and the bad with obstacles, so that they can never escape the equity of His judgment; and the good receive for their merits the glory and joy of life, and the bad the pain and grief of death, according to what God's vision sees in them.

How the Knowledge of God scrutinizes those clothed in a new garment

And the figure looks upon the people who come in from the world and in the build-ing put on a new garment. This is to say that the Knowledge of God knows those who leave the wickedness of infidelity and, by the power of God's work, put on the new self in baptism for the sake of eternal life. And she warns them not to turn backward and go toward the Devil, or, if they do thus stray, that they should return to God their Creator, as she says to each of them in the words of her admonition quoted above.

But let the one who has ears sharp to hear inner meanings ardently love My reflection, pant after My words, and inscribe them in his soul and conscience.

The New Heaven and the New Earth

After this I looked, and behold, all the elements and creatures were shaken by dire convulsions; fire and air and water burst forth, and the earth was made to move; lightning and thunder crashed, and mountains and forests fell; and all that was mortal expired. And all the elements were purified, and whatever had been foul in them vanished and was no more seen. And I heard a voice resounding in a great cry throughout the world, saying, "O ye children of men who are lying in the earth, rise up one and all!"

And behold, all the human bones in whatever place in the earth they lay were brought together in one moment and covered with their flesh; and they all rose up with limbs and bodies intact, each in his or her gender, with the good glowing brightly and the bad manifest in blackness, so that each one's deeds were openly seen. And some of them had been sealed with the sign of faith, but some had not; and some of those signed had a gold radiance about their faces, but others a shadow, which was their sign.

And suddenly from the east a great brilliance shone forth; and there, in a cloud, I saw the Son of Man, with the same appearance He had had in the world and with His wounds still open, coming with the angelic choirs. He sat upon a throne of flame, glowing but not burning, which floated on the great tempest that was purifying the world. And those who had been signed were taken up into the air to join Him as if by a whirlwind, to where I had previously seen the radiance that signifies the secrets of the Supernal Creator; and thus the good were separated from the bad. And, as the Gospel indicates, He blessed the just in a gentle voice and pointed them to the heavenly kingdom, and with a terrible voice condemned the unjust to the pains of Hell, *as is written in the same place.* Yet He made no inquiry or statement about their works except the words the Gospel declares would be made there; for each person's work, whether good or bad, showed clearly in him. But those who were not signed stood far off in the northern region, with the Devil's band; and they did not come to this judgment, but saw all these things in the whirlwind, and awaited the end of the judgment while uttering bitter groans.

And when the judgment was ended, the lightnings and thunders and winds and tempests ceased, the fleeting components of the elements vanished all at once, and there came an exceedingly great calm. And then the elect became more splendid than the splendor of the sun; and with great joy they made their way toward Heaven with the Son of God and the blessed armies of the angels. And at the same time the reprobate were forced with great howling toward the infernal regions with the Devil and his angels; and so Heaven received the elect, and Hell swallowed up the reprobate. And at once such great joy and praise arose in Heaven and such great misery and howling in Hell as were beyond human power to utter. And all the elements shone calm and resplendent, as if a black skin had been taken from them, so that fire no longer had its raging heat, or air density, or water turbulence, or earth shakiness. And the sun, moon, and stars sparkled in the firmament like great ornaments, remaining fixed and not moving in orbit, so that they no longer distinguished day from night. And so there was no night, but day. And it was finished.

And again I heard the voice from Heaven saying to me:

In the last days the world will be dissolved in disasters like a dying man

These mysteries manifest the last days, in which time will be transmuted into the eternity of perpetual light. For the last days will be

troubled by many dangers, and the end of the world will be prefigured by many signs. For, as you see, *on that last day the whole world will be
agitated by terrors and shaken by tempests, so that whatever is fleeting and mortal in it
will be ended.* For the course of the world is now complete, and it
cannot last longer, but will be consummated as God wills. For as a
person who is to die is captured and laid low by many infirmities
and in the hour of his death suffers great pain in his dissolution, so
too the greatest adversities will precede the end of the world and at
last dissolve it in terror. For the elements will then display their terrors, because they will not be able to do so afterward.

All creation will be moved and purified of all that is mortal in it

And so, at this consummation, *the elements are unloosed by a sudden and
unexpected movement:* all creatures are set into violent motion, fire
bursts out, the air dissolves, water runs off, the earth is shaken,
lightnings burn, thunders crash, mountains are broken, forests
fall, and whatever in air or water or earth is mortal gives up its
life. For the fire displaces all the air, and the water engulfs all the
earth; and thus all things are purified, and whatever was foul in
the world vanishes as if it had never been, as salt disappears
when it is put into water.

The bodies of the dead will rise again in their wholeness and gender

And when, as you saw, *the divine command to rise again resounds, the bones
of the dead, wherever they may be, are brought together in one moment and covered*

with their flesh. They will not be hindered by anything; but if they were consumed by fire or water or eaten by birds or beasts, they will be speedily restored. And so the earth will yield them up as salt is extracted from water; for My eye knows all things, and nothing can be hidden from Me. And so *all people will rise again in the twinkling of an eye, in soul and body, with no deformity or mutilation but intact in body and in gender; and the elect will shine with the brightness of their good works, but the reprobate will bear the blackness of their deeds of misery.* Thus their works will not there be concealed, but will appear in them openly.

The risen who are signed and unsigned

And some of them are sealed with the sign of faith, but some are not; and the consciences of some who have faith shine with the radiance of wisdom, but the consciences of others are murky from their neglect. And thus they are clearly distinguished; for the former have done the works of faith, but the latter have extinguished it in themselves. And those who do not have the sign of faith are those who chose not to know the living and true God either in the old Law or in the new Grace.

The Son will come to the judgment in human form

And then the Son of God, in the human form He had at His Passion when He suffered by the will of the Father to save the human race, will come to judge it, surrounded by the celestial army; He will be in the brightness of eternal life, but in the cloud that hides celestial glory from the reprobate. For the Father vouchsafed to Him the judging of the visible things of the world,

because He had lived visibly in the world, as He Himself shows
in the Gospel, saying:

The Gospel on this subject

"And He has given Him power to judge, because He is the Son
of Man" [John 5:27]. Which is to say: The Father has borne witness to His Son. What does this mean? The Father gave power to
the Son, because He remained with the Father in Divinity but
received humanity from a mother; and, because He is human,
He received also from the Father that every creature should feel
Him as the Son of God, for all creatures were created and formed
by God. And therefore all deeds will be judged by the Son, whatever their nobility or baseness, and He will put them in their
proper order. For, as He was a man palpable and visible in the
world, He can justly distinguish all that is visible in the world.
And He will appear in His power of judging terrible to the
unjust, but gentle to the just, and judge them so that the very
elements will feel the purgation.

The signed will be taken up easily to meet
their Judge

And those who are signed are taken up to meet the Just Judge not with difficulty but with great speed, so that in them, who had faith in
God, the works of faith may clearly be seen. And, as was shown
you, *the good are separated from the bad,* for their works are dissimilar.
For here it is apparent how both the bad and the good have
sought God in infancy, childhood, youth, and old age.

All God's flowers, the great heroes of the Church, will appear radiant

And here all the flowers of My Son will shine out in radiance, that is to say, the patriarchs and prophets who lived before His Incarnation; the apostles who lived with Him in the world; the martyrs, confessors, virgins, and widows who have faithfully imitated Him; the holders of high office, both secular and spiritual, in My Church; and the anchorites and monks who chastised and mortified their flesh and imitated the humility and charity of the angels in their garments, thus belittling themselves for My Son's name. Those who seek Me in the contemplative life because they think that life is more glorious than another are as nothing to Me; but any who seek Me in humility in that life because the Holy Spirit inspired them to do so I will put in the first ranks in the celestial homeland.

Amid the silence of Heaven, the Son will give sentence on all

Then the heavens will subdue their praises and remain awhile in silence, while the Son of God pronounces judicial sentence both on the just and on the unjust. And they will give ear with reverence and honor to how He decides; and *He will gently grant supernal joys to the just and terribly consign the unjust to the pains of Hell. And there will be no further excuses or questions about human works,* for here the consciences of both the good and the bad are naked and revealed.

Why the good and the bad need to be judged

Now the just, who will receive the words of the most equitable Judge, have indeed done many good works, but while they lived in the world they did not act with fullness of perfection, and therefore their deeds must now be judged. And the unjust, who will suffer a severe judgment against them, have indeed done much evil; but they did not act in ignorance of the Divine Majesty, in the wicked unbelief that would damn them without judgment. And so they will not escape the Judge's sentence, for all things must be weighed equitably.

Unbelievers are already judged and so will not come to the judgment

But those who are not signed in faith, because they did not believe in God, will tarry in the north, the region of perdition, with the Devil's band, and not come to this judgment. But they will see it all in obscurity and await its end, groaning deeply within themselves because they persevered in unbelief and did not know the true God. For they neither worshiped the Living God in the Old Testament before the institution of baptism, nor received the remedy of baptism in the Gospel, but continued under the curse of Adam's fall with its penalty of damnation. And therefore they are already judged for the crime of infidelity.

When the judgment is finished, a great calm will arise

And when the judgment is ended, the terrors of the elements, the lightnings and thunders and winds and tempests, will cease, and all that is fleeting and transitory will melt away and *no longer be*, like snow melted by the heat of the sun. *And so, by God's dispensation, an exceedingly great calm will arise.*

Glory will receive the elect, and Hell swallow up the damned

And thus the elect will become splendid with the splendor of eternity *and with My Son, their Head, and the glorious celestial army will embrace glory and the heavenly joys; while the reprobate, together with the Devil and his angels, will wretchedly direct their course toward eternal punishment,* where eternal death awaits them for following their lusts instead of My commands. *And so Heaven will receive the elect* into the glory of eternity, because they have loved the Ruler of the heavens; *and Hell will swallow up the reprobate,* because they did not renounce the Devil. *And then such great joy and praise will resound in the glory of Heaven and such great groaning and howling will arise in Hell as to exceed the grasp of the human understanding.* For the first have eternal life and the second eternal death, as My Son declares in the Gospel, saying:

The Gospel on this subject

"And these shall go into everlasting punishment; but the just into life everlasting" [Matt. 25:46]. Which is to say: Those who befoul themselves in the house of evil passions and do not thirst to drink justice from the Supreme Goodness will come, in the course of their infidelity and wickedness, to submersion in the pains of eternal perdition and according to their deeds will receive the torments of Hell. But the builders of the heavenly Jerusalem, who faithfully stand in the gates of the daughter of Zion, will be radiant in the eternal life, which the fruitfulness of the chaste Virgin miraculously gave to all believers.

How the elements and heavenly bodies will be changed, and night ended

And, as you see, when all these things are over *the elements will shine out with the greatest brightness and beauty, and all blackness and filth will be removed from them.* And fire, *without its raging heat,* will blaze like the dawn; *air without density* will be completely limpid; *water without its power to flood or drown* will stand transparent and calm; and *earth without shakiness* or roughness will be firm and level. And so all these will be transformed into great calm and beauty.

And *the sun, moon, and stars will sparkle in the* firmament like precious stones set in gold, with great glory and brilliance; and *they will no longer restlessly revolve in orbit* so as to distinguish day from night. For the world will have ended and they will have become immutable; and from that time on *there will be no darkness, and day will be perpetual,* as My beloved John witnesses, when he says:

Words of John

"And there shall be no more night, and they will not need the light of the lamp or the light of the sun; for the Lord God will illumine them" [Rev. 22:5]. Which is to say: One who possesses a treasure sometimes hides it and at other times shows it, and even so night conceals the light, and day drives out the darkness and brings light to humanity. But it will not be so when time is transformed; for then the shade of night will be put to flight and its darkness will not appear from that time on. For in this transmutation the light people now light to dispel the darkness will not be needed; and the sun will not move and by its motion bring times of darkness. For then the day will be without end; for the Ruler of all, in the immutable glory of His Divinity, will illumine those who in the world have by His grace escaped the darkness.

But let the one who has ears sharp to hear inner meanings ardently love My reflection, pant after My words, and inscribe them in his soul and conscience.

Symphony of the Blessed

Then I saw the lucent sky, in which I heard different kinds of music, marvelously embodying all the meanings I had heard before. I heard the praises of the joyous citizens of Heaven, steadfastly persevering in the ways of truth; and laments calling people back to those praises and joys; and the exhortations of the virtues, spurring one another on to secure the salvation of the peoples ensnared by the Devil. And the virtues destroyed his snares, so that the faithful at last through repentance passed out of their sins and into Heaven.

And their song, like the voice of a multitude, making music in harmony praising the ranks of Heaven, had these words:

Songs to holy Mary

O splendid jewel, serenely infused with the Sun!
The Sun is in you as a fount from the heart of the Father;
It is His sole Word, by whom He created the world,
The primary matter, which Eve threw into disorder.
He formed the Word in you as a human being,
And therefore you are the jewel that shines most brightly,
Through whom the Word breathed out the whole of the virtues,
As once from primary matter He made all creatures.

O sweet green branch that flowers from the stem of Jesse!
O glorious thing, that God on His fairest daughter
Looked as the eagle looks on the face of the sun!

The Most High Father sought for a Virgin's candor,
And willed that His Word should take in her His body.
For the Virgin's mind was by His mystery illumined,
And from her virginity sprang the glorious Flower.
And again a song resounded:

To the nine orders of heavenly spirits

   O glorious Living Light, which lives in Divinity!
Angels who fix your eyes with ardent desire
Amid the mystical darkness surrounding all creatures
On Him with whom your desires can never be sated!
O glorious joy, to live in your form and nature!
For you are free from every deed of evil,
Although that evil first appeared in your comrade,
The fallen angel, who tried to soar above God,
And therefore that twisted one was submerged in ruin.
And then for himself a greater fall he prepared
By his suggestions to those whom God's hand made.

   O angels with shining faces who guard the people,
O ye archangels, who take just souls into Heaven,
And you, O virtues and powers, O principalities,
Dominions and thrones, who by five are secretly counted,
And you, cherubim and seraphim, seal of God's secrets,
Praise be to you all, who behold the heart of the Father,
And see the Ancient of Days spring forth in the fountain,

And His inner power appear like a face from His heart.
And again they sang:

To the patriarchs and prophets

O eminent men, who traversed the hidden ways,
And looked with the eyes of the spirit, and in lucent shadows
Announced the Living Light that would bud from the stem
Which blossomed alone from the Light that rooted within it!
O ancient saints, you foretold the souls' salvation
Who were sunk in death; like wheels you turned and circled,
And wondrously spoke of the Mount that touches Heaven.
And then He came, and anointed the many waters,
And so the shining light arose among you,
And, going before Him, displayed the Mount Himself.

O happy roots, from whom miracles and not vices
Grew in the burning way of lucent shadow!
And you, O fiery voice of meditation
Who went before the abyss-sealing Cornerstone;
Rejoice in your Head, in the One Whom so many among you
Invoked with ardor, yet never on earth beheld.
And another song was sung:

To the apostles

O warrior cohort of the thornless Flower!
Your sound fills the world, traversing the realm of the senses,

Where madmen feast and defile themselves with swine;
And you, infused with the Comforter, conquered them.
O noble race of the Savior, whose roots are fixed
In the tabernacle of the Word's complete labor,
You take by the Lamb the path of the water's salvation.
He sent you armed with a sword amid dogs most savage,
Who with the work of their fingers destroyed their glory,
Subjecting the Handlessly Made to their hands' own makings.

O lucent crowd of apostles, in truest knowledge
You rose to open the Devil's mighty prisons
And cleanse his slaves in the fount of living waters.
You are the glorious light in the blackest darkness,
The pillars that prop the jeweled Bride of the Lamb,
Whose banner-bearer first was the Virgin Mother,
For joy of the Lamb, who weds the immaculate Bride.
And another song resounded:

To the martyrs

O ye who have poured out your blood in triumph,
And conquered a share in the blood of the Lamb who perished,
Feasting upon the slain calf's sacrifice,
And so built the Church, what a great reward is yours!
Alive, you followed the Lamb, and despised your bodies,
Adorned His pains, and so recaptured your portions.

O rose blossoms, blessed in the joy of your blood's effusion!
Your fragrant blood flowed forth from the inner counsel
Of Him who has been always, without beginning,
And planned before time began His great redemption.
    Your company is honor, whose blood abounded
To build the Church in the stream from your noble wounds.
And another song was sung:

To the confessors

O ye who succeed and serve the mighty Lion,
And rule between the temple and the altar,
The angels sing praises and stand to help the peoples,
And so do you, in the Lamb's service careful.

O ye who imitate the Most Exalted,
In His most precious and glorious Sacrament!
How great is your glory, in which the power is given
To loose and bind the indolent and the straying,
To beautify white and black, and lift their burdens.
    Yours too is the office of the angelic order,
And yours is the task of knowing the firm foundations
And where to lay them; and therefore great is your honor.
And another song resounded:

To the virgins

O lovely faces who look on the face of God
And build in the dawn; O noble blessed virgins!

The King took thought for you, sealing you to His purpose
And decking you with all ornaments of Heaven,
And so you are a garden adorned in sweetness.

   O noble verdure, which grows from the Sun of splendor!
Your clear serenity shines in the Wheel of Godhead,
Your greatness is past all earthly understanding,
And Heaven's wonders surround you in their embrace.
   You glow like dawn, and burn like the Sun in glory.
*And another song was heard, like the voice of a multitude breaking out in melodic
laments over the people who had to be brought back to that place:*

The lament over the ones to be recalled
   Oh, this is a voice of sorrow and great lamenting!
Ah! ah! what a wonderful victory has arisen:
The desire for God, while carnal pleasure flees!
But oh, alas! how few were the wills that were sinless,
How few the desires that fled from lust to You!
Mourn, mourn then, Innocence, you whose modest goodness
Has never failed, nor craved what the Serpent showed you,
For people respected, though they neglected you.

   O Living Fountain, how great is Your sweet compassion!
You never lost sight of the face of the straying people,
But saw in advance the way that You would save them
From the fallen angels, who thought they had reft them
from You.

O daughter of Zion, rejoice that God restores you
So many cut off from you by the ancient serpent,
Who now shine brighter than ever they shone before.

    The Living Light now says of the ones He rescued,
"The guileful serpent I flouted in his seduction,
His work was not so perfect as once he thought it.
I swore by Myself, and I did more, far more,
For them than he did to them. And so your joy
Is ended, your snares destroyed, and all your greed
Is come to nothing, O wickedest of impostors!"

And again a song was heard, like the voice of a multitude, exhorting the virtues to help humanity and oppose the inimical arts of the Devil. And the virtues overcame the vices, and by divine inspiration people turned back to repentance. And thus the song resounded in harmony:

The exhortation of the virtues and the fight against the Devil

THE VIRTUES: We virtues are in God, and there abide; we wage war for the King of Kings, and separate evil from good. We appeared in the first battle and conquered there, while the one who tried to fly above himself fell. So let us now wage war and help those who invoke us; let us tread underfoot the Devil's arts and guide those who would imitate us to the blessed mansions.

SOULS (in the body, lamenting): Oh, we are strangers, wandering off toward sin! What have we done? We should have been daughters of the King, but we fell into the darkness of sin. O living Sun, carry us on Your shoulders into the just inheritance, which we lost in Adam! O King of Kings, let us fight in your battle!

A FAITHFUL SOUL: O sweet Divinity and O lovely Life, in whom I may put on a robe of glory and receive what I lost in the beginning! I long for You, and I call upon the virtues.

VIRTUES (answering): O blessed soul! O sweet creature of God, who was formed in the depths of God's profound wisdom, you have loved much.

THE SOUL: Oh, I come to you gladly; give me the kiss of the heart!

VIRTUES: We must join with you in the battle, O daughter of the King.

THE SOUL (burdened and complaining): Oh, burdensome labor! Oh, heavy load I must endure while garbed in this life! It is most hard for me to fight against the flesh.

VIRTUES: O soul created by God's will, O happy instrument! Why are you so weak against the thing God has crushed by the Virgin? Through us you must conquer the Devil.

THE SOUL: Help, support me, that I may stand firm!

KNOWLEDGE OF GOD: See what it is that you are clothed with, O daughter of salvation, and stand firm! Then you will never fall.

THE SOUL: Oh, I know not what to do or where to flee! Woe is me! I cannot use rightly that which clothes me. I want to tear it off!

VIRTUES: O bad conscience, O wretched soul! Why do you hide your face in the presence of your Creator?

KNOWLEDGE OF GOD: You do not know or see or taste Him who created you.

THE SOUL: God created the world; I do Him no wrong if I want to enjoy it.

THE DEVIL (whispering to the soul): Fool, fool! What good is your labor? Regard the world, and it will embrace you with honor.

VIRTUES: Alas, alas! Virtues, let us loudly lament and mourn, for a sheep of the Lord is fleeing from life.

HUMILITY: I, Humility, queen of the virtues, say: Come to me, all of you virtues, and I will strengthen you, so that you can seek the lost coin and give it the crown of blessed perseverance!

VIRTUES: O glorious queen, O sweetest mediator! We come gladly.

HUMILITY: Beloved daughters, I keep you in the King's wedding chamber. O daughters of Israel, God raised you under His tree, so now remember your planting. Rejoice, O daughters of Zion!

THE DEVIL (to the Virtues): What good is it that there should be no power but God's? I say that I will give everything to the one who follows me and his own will; but you and all your followers have nothing to give, for none of you knows who you are.

HUMILITY: I and my companions know well that you are the ancient dragon, who tried to fly higher than the Most High, and was thrown into the deepest abyss by God Himself.

VIRTUES: But all of us dwell on high.

THE SOUL (in the body, repentant and lamenting): O royal virtues! How beautifully you shine in the Supreme Sun! How sweet is your dwelling! Oh, woe is me, I fled from you!

VIRTUES: Come, O fugitive, come to us! And God will receive you.

THE SOUL: Alas, alas! Burning sweetness plunged me into sins; I dare not enter with you.

VIRTUES: Do not fear or flee; the Good Shepherd seeks you, His lost sheep.

THE SOUL: Now I need you to take me back, for I fester with wounds the ancient serpent has dealt me.

VIRTUES: Run to us, and follow with us that path in which you will never fall; and God will heal you.

THE SOUL: I am a sinner who fled from Life; I must come to you full of sores, that you may offer me the shield of redemption.

VIRTUES: O fugitive soul, be firm, and put on yourself the armor of light!

THE SOUL: O soldiery of the Queen, O white lilies and crimson roses, look gently upon me! I have lived as a stranger and an exile from you; help me to rise up in the blood of the Son of God! O Humility, who are true healing, help me; for Pride has broken me with many vices and wounded me with many scars. Now I fly to you; oh, receive me!

HUMILITY (to the Virtues): O virtues all, for the sake of Christ's wounds receive this mourning sinner, scarred as she is, and bring her to me.

VIRTUES (to the Soul): We will bring you back, and we will not desert you; the whole celestial army rejoices over you! And so we will sing a song of rejoicing.

HUMILITY (to the Soul): O unhappy daughter, I will embrace you; for the great Physician for your sake suffered deep and bitter wounds.

THE DEVIL (whispering to the Soul): Who are you, and whence do you come? You embraced me, and I led you forth; and now you return and confound me! But I will throw you down in battle.

THE SOUL (to the Devil): I recognized that all your ways are evil, and so I fled from you. And now, O impostor, I fight against you! (To Humility): O Queen Humility, help me with your healing remedy!

HUMILITY (to Victory and the other Virtues): O Victory! You conquered the Devil in Heaven; run now with your companions, and all bind this Devil!

VICTORY (to the Virtues): O strong and glorious soldiers, come and help me conquer this deceiver!

VIRTUES (to Victory): O sweetest warrior in the flowing fountain that engulfed the ravenous wolf! O you crowned with glory, we gladly fight with you against the deluder of souls.

HUMILITY: Bind him, O splendid virtues!

VIRTUES: O queen, we will obey you, and do your commands in all things.

VICTORY: Rejoice, comrades! The ancient serpent is bound!

VIRTUES: Praise be to you, O Christ, King of the angels! O God, who are You who had this great counsel in You? It destroyed the hellish drink, which poisoned the publicans and sinners; and they now shine in celestial goodness. Praise therefore be to You, O King! O Father Almighty, from Your ardent heat flows the fountain; guide your children with a favorable wind on the waters, that we may lead them into the celestial Jerusalem.

And these voices were like the voices of a multitude lifting up its sound on high.

And their song went through me, so that I understood them perfectly.

And I heard a voice from the shining sky saying to me:

God must be unceasingly praised for His grace with heart and voice

Praises must be offered unceasingly to the Supernal Creator with heart and mouth, for by His grace he sets on heavenly thrones not only those who stand erect, but those who bend and fall.

Thus, O human, you see the lucent sky, which symbolizes the brilliance of the joy of the citizens of Heaven, in which you hear different kinds of music, marvelously embodying all the meanings you heard before. You hear the praises of the joyous citizens of Heaven, steadfastly persevering in the ways of truth, and laments calling people back to those praises and joys. For, as the air encloses and sustains everything under the heavens, so the wonders of God, which you have already been shown, are enveloped for you in a sweet and delightful song. It sings with joy of the wonders of the elect who dwell in the heavenly city and eternally express their sweet devotion to God; and it laments over the wavering of those the ancient serpent is trying to destroy, but who will be led to blessed joy by the divine power and know the mysteries no human mind can know that bows down to the earth.

And you hear the exhortations of the virtues, spurring one another on to secure the salvation of the peoples ensnared by the Devil; and the virtues destroy his snares, so that the faithful at last through repentance pass out of their sins and into Heaven. For the virtues in the minds of the faithful resist the vices by which the Devil wearies them and redeem them; and when their mighty strength conquers these vices, the people who fell into sin return by God's will to repentance, diligently examining and weeping over their former deeds and weighing and considering their future ones.

The song is sung in unity and concord

And so that song, like the voice of a multitude, makes music in praise among the ranks of Heaven. For the song of rejoicing, sung in consonance and in concord, tells of the glory and honor of the citizens of Heaven and lifts on high what the Word has shown.

The words are the body and the music the spirit

And so the words symbolize the body, and the jubilant music indicates the spirit; the celestial harmony shows the Divinity, and the words the Humanity of the Son of God.

By this song the sluggish soul is aroused to watchfulness

And as the power of God is everywhere and encompasses all things, and no obstacle can stand against it, so too the human intellect has great power to resound in living voices and arouse sluggish souls to vigilance by the song.

David shows this by his songs of prophecy and rejoicing, and Jeremiah shows it by the sorrowful voice of his lamentation. And you also, O human, with your poor and frail little nature, can hear in the song the ardor of virginal modesty embraced by the blossoming branch; the acuity of the living lights, which shine in the heavenly city; the profound utterances of the apostles; the outpouring of the blood of the faithful who offer themselves; the secrets of the priestly office; and the procession of virgins, blooming in the verdancy of Heaven. For the faithful creature rejoices to his Creator in a voice of exultation and gladness and returns Him perpetual gratitude. *And you hear another song, like the voice of a multitude breaking out in melodic laments over the people who have to be brought back to that place.* For the song does not only harmonize and exult over those who persevere in the path of rectitude, but also exults in the concord of those who are resurrected from their fall out of the path of justice and are at last uplifted to true beatitude. For the Good Shepherd has brought back to the fold with joy the sheep that was lost.

And again you hear a song, like the voice of a multitude, exhorting the virtues to help humanity and oppose the arts of the Devil. And the virtues overcome the vices, and by divine inspiration people turn back to repentance; and so their song resounds in harmony. For the sweet alliance of the virtues draws the faithful to true beatitude, though the vices the Devil uses as snares accumulate direly. But the virtues do not merely conquer the vices, but destroy them; and so they lead people who consent to be helped by God to eternal reward by true penitence. And this is shown by the words of their song.

The song of rejoicing softens the hard heart and summons the Holy Spirit

For the song of rejoicing softens hard hearts, draws forth from them the tears of compunction, and invokes the Holy Spirit. *And so those voices you hear are like the voice of a multitude, which lifts its sound on* high; for jubilant praises, offered in simple harmony and charity, lead the faithful to that consonance in which is no discord, and make those who still live on earth sigh with heart and voice for the heavenly reward.

And their song goes through you so that you understand them perfectly; for where divine grace has worked, it banishes all dark obscurity and makes pure and lucid those things that are obscure to the bodily senses because of the weakness of the flesh.

The faithful should rejoice without ceasing

Therefore, let everyone who understands God by faith faithfully offer Him tireless praises and with joyful devotion sing to Him without ceasing, as My servant David, filled with the spirit of lofty profundity, exhorts on My behalf, saying:

Words of David

"Praise Him with the sound of trumpets; praise Him with psaltery and harp. Praise Him with timbrel and dance; praise Him with stringed instruments and flute. Praise Him on high-sounding cymbals; praise Him on cymbals of joy; let every spirit praise the Lord" [Ps. 150:3–6]. This is to say: You know, adore, and love God with simple mind and pure devotion. Praise Him, then, with the sound of trumpets, which is to say by the use of the reason. For when the lost angel and his consenters fell into perdition, the armies of the blessed spirits stood firm in the truth of reason and with faithful devotion adhered to God.

And praise Him on the psaltery of deep devotion and the honey-toned harp. For when the trumpet sounds, the psaltery follows, and when the psaltery sounds, the harp follows; as first the blessed angels stood fast in the love of truth, then after the creation of Man the prophets arose with their wonderful voices, and then the apostles followed with their words of sweetness.

And praise Him with the timbrel of mortification and in the dance of exultation. For after the harp sounds, the timbrel exults, and after the timbrel, the dance; as after the apostles preached words of salvation, the martyrs endured many bodily torments for the honor of God, and then arose the truthful doctors of the priestly office.

And praise Him with the stringed instruments of human redemption and the flute of divine protection. For after the dance of joy, the voice of the stringed instruments and the flute emerge; as, after the doctors who served beatitude showed the truth, there appeared the virgins, who loved the Son of God, who was true Man, like stringed instruments and adored Him, who was true God, like flutes. For they believed Him to be true Man and true God. What does this mean? When the Son of God assumed flesh for human salvation, He did not lose the glory of Divinity; and so the happy virgins chose Him as their Bridegroom, and knew Him with faithful devotion as true Man in betrothal and true God in chastity.

And praise Him too on high-sounding cymbals, which is to say by loud and joyful declarations, whenever people who lay in the depths of sin are touched by divinely inspired remorse and raise themselves from those depths to the height of Heaven. And praise Him on cymbals of joy, which is to say by statements of praise, whenever the strong virtues gain the victory, overthrow human vice, and lead people who persevere in good works and holy desires to the beatitude of the true recompense. And so let every spirit who wills to believe in God and honor Him praise the Lord, Him who is the Lord of all; for it is fitting that anyone who desires life should glorify Him who is Life.

And again I heard a voice from the lucent sky saying: "O King most high, praise be to You, who bring these things to pass in a simple and untaught person!"

And another voice cried out from Heaven with a great shout, saying:

Hear and attend, all you who desire to have heavenly recompense and bliss. O ye people who have believing hearts and await the heavenly reward, take these words and lay them up in your inmost hearts, and do not reject this admonition that comes to you. For I the Living and True Witness of Truth, the speaking and not silent God, say and say again: Who shall prevail over Me? He who tries it I will overthrow. Let not anyone lay hold of a mountain, which he cannot move, but let him abide in the valley of humility. Who walks a road without water? The one who is swayed by the whirlwind and divides fruit but does not eat it. And how can My tabernacle be there? My tabernacle is the place where the Holy Spirit pours forth Its overflowing waters. What does this mean?

I am in the midst. How? Whoever lays hold of Me worthily shall not fall, either as to height or as to depth or as to breadth. What does this mean?

I am that Charity which emulous pride cannot cast down, a fall into the depths cannot dash to pieces, and the wide expanse of evils cannot crush. Can I not build as high as the footstool of the sun? The strong despise Me, who show their strength in the valleys; the apathetic leave me at the sound of the tempest; the learned refuse My food; and so do they all who build towers for themselves according to their own will. But I will confound them through the small and the weak, as I overthrew Goliath by a boy and conquered Holofernes by Judith. And therefore, if anyone rejects the mystical words of this book, I will draw My bow against him and transfix him by the arrows from My quiver; I will knock his crown from his head and make him like those who fell in Horeb when they murmured against Me. And if anyone utters curses against this prophecy, may the curse that Isaac uttered come upon him. But anyone who embraces it, keeps it in his heart, and makes its ways plain, I will fill with the dews of Heaven.

And whoever tastes this prophecy and fixes it in his memory will become the mountain of myrrh, frankincense, and all aromatic spices and the diffusion of many blessings; he will ascend like Abraham from blessing to blessing. And the new spouse, the Bride of the Lamb, will take him to herself, for he is a pillar in the sight of God. And the shadow of the hand of the Lord will protect him.

But whoever rashly conceals these words written by the finger of God, madly abridging them or for any human reason taking them to a strange place and scoffing at them, let him be reprobate; and the finger of God shall crush him.

Praise, therefore, praise God, ye blessed hearts, for the miracles God has wrought in the frail earthly reflection of the beauty of the Most High, as He Himself foreshadowed when He first made Woman from the rib of the man He had created.

But let the one who has ears sharp to hear inner meanings ardently love My reflection, pant after My words, and inscribe them in his soul and conscience. Amen.

ABOUT THE EDITOR

HarperCollins Spiritual Classics Series Editor Emilie Griffin has long been interested in the classics of the devotional life. She has written a number of books on spiritual formation and transformation, including *Clinging: The Experience of Prayer* and *Wilderness Time: A Guide to Spiritual Retreat*. With Richard J. Foster she coedited *Spiritual Classics: Selected Readings on the Twelve Spiritual Disciplines*. Her latest book is *Wonderful and Dark Is this Road: Discovering the Mystic Path*. She is a board member of Renovaré and leads retreats and workshops throughout the United States. She and her husband, William, live in Alexandria, Louisiana.

ABOUT HOMER HICKAM

Homer Hickam is the bestselling author of *Rocket Boys* (aka *October Sky*), *The Coalwood Way*, *The Ambassador's Son*, and many other books. For more information, please see www.homerhickam.com.